The Popcorn Cathedral

ROD BENNETT

ISBN-13:
978-1533235497

ISBN-10:
153323549X

DEDICATION

To my daughter
MARTHA CLARE BENNETT

Always curious about words

CONTENTS

Author's Introduction

Jesus was my first love.

Later on, I added film—especially fantasy films.

Working out the hierarchy wasn't actually difficult: "He is before all things, and by him all things consist…who is the beginning, the firstborn from the dead; that in all things he might have the preeminence" (Col 1:17-18). Working out exactly how this other love might fit in anyway—*that's* what has taken the bigger part of a lifetime.

For a long time I thought being a Christian first meant being a Christian *instead.*

When, in other words, one detects an urge to watch *Citizen Kane* or *Lost Horizon* or *7th Voyage of Sinbad*, one should go to church instead. Or give out some gospel tracts door-to-door. Read the Bible. Anyhow, every minute watching a movie was a minute stolen from God. (I soon learned that nobody actually lives this way; the golf fanatic may go to church an awful lot…but he rarely stops playing golf. He plays anyway and just feels guilty about it). Under the pressure of this idea, I sometimes threw away my movie posters, *Star Wars* magazines, and film books—it was regular fit that came over me from time to time. After all, you have to choose. Later, my film buff friends and I (mostly fellow Christians) began to call this the "God or Godzilla?" dilemma.

Only much later did I realize that being a "Christian first" meant being a Christian first *in everything*…a Christian first *as* a film fan. Christ was to be Lord *over* your life, not instead of your life. And I soon rejoiced to find no less an authority than C.S. Lewis seconding this emotion: "What we need is not more little books about Christianity, but more little books by Christians on other subjects—with their Christianity latent." That's where these little essays and stories came in…

Most are about movies (the others, about fantasy subjects on the periphery of this passion). Others use movies to make spiritual or even political points. One of them is actually pretty technical (*Jurassic Park and the Death of Stop-Motion Animation*—which came out right at the very start of today's computer graphics revolution and was praised for its insight, I'm pleased to report, by *Jurassic Park*'s effects supervisor himself). All of them appeared prior to the publication of my first book, *Four Witnesses; The Early Church in Her Own Words.*

If you, at any rate, happen to find *yourself* living "at the junction of film, faith, and fantasy" I'm certain you'll discover something here to enjoy.

Rod Bennett

Tariffville, Tennessee

THE GOSPEL ACCORDING TO FRANK CAPRA

At Christmastime in the year 1974, when I was 14 years old, I saw an old black & white movie on television called *It's A Wonderful Life*. It was a very cold sunny afternoon as I remember; I was home from school on two weeks of Christmas vacation. I had been randomly turning the TV dial and just happened to get interested in a scene -- about ten minutes into the picture, as it turns out -- in which a young boy had just saved a drunken druggist from accidentally poisoning a sick child. At the first commercial break, the "Armchair Theatre" announcer told me the title.

Wracked as I was at the time with all the usual terrors and traumas of being fourteen years old, I wasn't at all sure that it was, in fact, a wonderful life here on Planet Earth. But I watched the movie anyway. And the longer that old picture went on the more the sound of that title (which had seemed at first so pat and sugary) began to change in my doubtful ears. *It's A Wonderful Life*. Standing there so unashamed in the face of everything going on all around it, that simplistic, illogical phrase began to sound... I don't know... defiant; like a challenge being flung at me or even an *attack*.

I had no way of knowing at the time that this was supposed to be a corny old Christmas "feel-good" movie. It began to make me feel pretty bad, in fact. Certainly I saw that *It's A Wonderful Life* is full of wonderful things: charm and humor and unforgettable characters that have since become like a second family to me. But the longer the movie went on, the bleaker and blacker things got. George Bailey, the hero (played by James Stewart), the dreamer who was going to see the world and lasso the moon, struggles to get out of the dead end job that keeps him chained to the hick town where he was born. It soon becomes obvious, to us and to him, that he never will get out of it. And yet, somehow, with every commercial break, that announcer kept repeating *It's A Wonderful Life.* I myself had dreams very like George Bailey's: dreams of accomplishment, dreams of romance. But the plain reality was that I was failing in school, my first real romance was ten years away, and I was lonely, alienated, and ugly with that unique ugliness only possible to fourteen year olds. And yet with every commercial break, over and over at eight-minute intervals, the "Armchair Theatre" man insisted *It's A Wonderful Life.* Before long, George Bailey (because of a meaningless accident—his lovable, doddering old uncle has destroyed his business by absentmindedly losing a packet of money) stands on a frigid overpass ready to drown his whole thwarted, aborted dream in an icy black river and we're not so sure we blame him. I stood there with him—my own dreams seemed (and sometimes still seem) just as hopeless. And still the man says *It's A Wonderful Life.*

I guess the repeated words of that corny title—proved surely to be a lie by the very story to which they had somehow been tacked—made me feel a little like Nero must have felt, listening in disbelief to the joyful hymns the martyrs sang as he fed them to the lions.

And then the final act of the movie began.

With a cosmic zoom the whole scale of the story changes—our perspective becomes eternal. George Bailey's plain homely little life is suddenly revealed (by a frightening side-trip to a dark alternative universe) to have been all along part of a reality which includes within its boundaries vistas so vast and dangers so deep that the thought of it seems, by turns, far too god to be true and far too frightening to entertain. George receives, in the words of an angel, "... a great gift...the chance to see what the world would be like without you." It's a gift of gravestones, a gift of dark and desperate glimpses into "awful holes"; but when the vision has passed, our minds have been expanded. We realize we have sinned. We have agreed with George Bailey; his shabby small-town existence is a bore. And thus when the sheer bottomless profundity of every tiny detail of that life yawns before us—Zuzu's pitiful flower petals, for instance—we are ashamed. We suddenly know forever that George Bailey really was "the richest man in town." We see what we should have see all along; that five minutes in the presence of such as Bert the Bop, Ernie the Taxi Driver, Cousin Eustace and Uncle Billy...one drink at Martini's bar, one kiss from Mary Hatch, one hug from little Zuzu—each of these things has been a staggering unmerited honor worth any price.

To me it was a staggering vision. The man had been right. It was indeed, by God, a wonderful life.

I remember sitting stunned—battered by a bewildering rush of conflicting emotions as the closing credits finished and for some reason the

TV station wanted to go on now and show something else. What the hell had just happened to me? Why was I crying? Was I happy? Was I sad? Was this love or despair or what? I looked slowly around the room; everything looked the same as it had two hours before. But I knew I wasn't the same. Maybe I had taken the whole thing too seriously somehow. Maybe I just hadn't seen many movies yet. Maybe when you get older you get used to being slapped around like this. And probably that old movie doesn't show life as it really is. There probably aren't any angels and when the George Bailey's of the world get to the end of their ropes they just go ahead and drop off. It occurred to me that probably the whole thing was just a Hollywood fantasy. But then I found another voice rising up inside me –"In that case, Hollywood has paid us a compliment we don't deserve; it has made man seem far more grand and sad and glorious than he is. But if this is so, then who, if not a man, made this old movie?"

I wandered somehow into the family room of our house and collapsed into a big brown wing-backed chair. I'm sitting in it now as I write; I've kept the scarred old thing long after my parents discarded it because of the memory of that moment. It had gotten dark outside while I was watching the movie and so I sat there quietly, the room lit only by the rainbow twinkling of our Christmas tree and the warm yellow blaze in our fireplace. Before long, my folks came in, engaged in the usual Christmas hustle and bustle. I'm sure the look on my face must have been precisely the look George Bailey wears as he sees Tommy and Janey and Pete again for the first time after returning from "Never-Born-Land." After all, I had gone there with him. I had lost my family when George lost his family and regained them when, with George, I realized that it is, in very point of fact, a wonderful life. I hugged both of my parents as if I hadn't seen them in years. I didn't even try to explain what had happened to me; how could I? I'm sure they thought I was on drugs, which I felt like I was. Yet with the joy *It's A Wonderful Life* brought there came a new fear. Or perhaps it would be better to say a new challenge. Some people say (they've been saying it since 1946) "*It's A Wonderful Life* shows that every person's life turns out okay in the end." It doesn't. *It's A Wonderful Life* shows that George Bailey's turns out okay in the end; and George Bailey is really not such a common "common man." After all, if Mr. Potter (or even the man who pushes Mr. Potter's wheelchair) had been shown Bedford Falls as it would have been if he'd never been born, he'd have seen a far different picture than George sees (which, by the way, is the plot of Dickens' *A Christmas Carol*). I saw clearly that George Bailey's life was wonderful because he was wonderful – wonderfully and exceptionally good. It's not circumstance or fate that keeps George chained to his "shabby little office." He has had one grand opportunity after another to leave town: a ticket to college, $2000 for a honeymoon, Sam Wainwright's "ground floor in plastics," Mr. Potter's

$20,000 a year. George stays stuck in his hick town for one reason only—he cannot bring himself to sell his soul to get out of it. Though he doesn't know it (indeed, he can only see himself as a sucker for having done it) George has sold his dreams to keep Bedford Falls from becoming Pottersville. *It's A Wonderful Life* is a passion play; George Bailey's sufferings have saved all those he loves best; he loses his dream so that Martini and Mary and Violet Bick and Uncle Billy may have theirs. George Bailey's love has been his defeat and his defeat has been his victory. When the tests came "Slacker George... the miserable failure" was able to do the Greatest Thing in the World; Greater love hath no man than this—that he lay down his life for his friends.

So there was the new fear—the haunting question that frightened and fascinated me as I sat there with the tears welling in my eyes and the strange look on my face and my parents blaming the whole thing on hormones. "What about me? What about my life? What would I see if Clarence the Angel showed me what the world would be like without me?" I knew that I was not good; I wasn't much like George Bailey at all. "When this young life of mine is finished, will it turn out to have been as wonderful as George's or as pointless as Potter's?" And the answer seemed to come back—"It will be whatever you most want it to be. Blessed are they who hunger and thirst after righteousness for they shall have what they desire." That cheesy, corny title really had flung me a challenge: there's a sense in which my whole life has been an attempt to live up to that cold December afternoon in 1974.

At any rate, the purpose of this little bit of autobiography has been to point out that I was, as you may have noticed, rather badly shaken up by this old film that everyone else seems to find so mild and safe. I had no way of knowing, in my simplicity, that *It's A Wonderful Life* is old-fashioned, sentimental, and preaches an easy, cheap optimism. It seemed to me a rather horrifyingly costly optimism: take up your cross, for whoever clings to his life will lose it, but whoever lays down his life will save it unto life eternal.

Daniel in the Critic's Den

Not long after my Christmas encounter with *It's A Wonderful Life*, I took a trip to Tennessee to visit my grandmother. Once again, I found myself in front of the television, searching through the channels. Finding out what's playing on Channel Six or Ten or Twenty-Three (all those numbers that bring in nothing but static in your own hometown) was always a favorite activity there. Engaged in this pastime, my heart suddenly leapt as the spinning dial landed at a shot of George Bailey stumbling joyfully down the garlanded main street of Bedford Falls and wishing a Merry Christmas to his wonderful old Building and Loan. After a moment or two, I realized that this was not another showing of *It's A Wonderful Life* (which would have been welcomed, of course, then as I do now) but an hour-long American Film Institute documentary playing on a snowy Public TV station out of Chattanooga or someplace. As I watched this program, thrilled and curious, I learned the answer to at least one of the questions I had pondered after my first meeting with George Bailey—a man had indeed made *It's A Wonderful Life*. His name was Frank Capra and this was a show about his life and works. I eagerly swallowed and digested every scrap of information, amazed to learn that other people had also seen my special movie and remembered it. And even more amazing—one by one they showed scenes from and commented upon a whole litany of other Frank Capra movies! There were *others* where *It's A Wonderful Life* came from! I grabbed up a stubby pencil and wrote the titles on the back of an envelope: *Mr. Smith Goes to Washington, Lost Horizon, You Can't Take It With You, Mr. Deeds Goes to Town, Meet John Doe*. The titles are well known to film fans, but the list was like a treasure map to me.

As I sought and encountered these films over the next four or five years, my own experience of Capra remained just as comically at odds with his sweetsie reputation. Bosley Crowther of the *Times* had called *It's A Wonderful Life* "a figment of simple Pollyanna platitudes," and *The New Yorker* had declared the picture "... so mincing as to border on baby talk." The film had seemed to me so profound as to nearly defy analysis. Of course, I had never heard of *The New Yorker* or of Bosley Crowther, just as I had never heard of *It's A Wonderful Life*. I knew nothing of film or filmmakers or film criticism. I had watched *It's A Wonderful Life* with the wide eyes and wide open heart so characteristic of the completely ignorant. But surely there's something very strange about a movie that sounds like baby talk to one person and feels like a punch in the nose to another.

Before long I began to wonder if these critics and I were seeing the same films. *Meet John Doe* "lacked inspiration" according to *The Los Angeles Times*. I stayed up till three AM on a school night to see it and then lay awake thinking about it until the alarm went off that morning. Few movies classified as comedies (and they are very, very funny—only Preston Sturges did it as well), I was sure doing a lot of crying. I saw *Lost Horizon* in the cool depths of a marvelous old repertoire theater in Atlanta, now sadly gone with a yogurt store standing on it's gravesite. As the lights came up, I sat ravished in my seat with Dimitri Tiomkin's weird score ringing in my ears—and hearing the man sitting behind me suddenly ask his date if she'd "ever seen a stupider movie" is the closest I've ever come to believing John Calvin's doctrine of Limited Atonement. I had been told that *Mr. Deeds Goes to Town* is a glib piece of populist propaganda. I rather resented that as I sat weeping through a distressingly little parable about innocence betrayed without having adequately prepared myself. Later, I found that almost all the criticism ever written about this obviously spiritual film is economic; people of the left find *Mr. Deeds* entirely too capitalistic and those on the other side damn it as socialism. At this point, I began to suspect that it might be the critics rather than the films that were defective. I had never heard the word "Capra-corn;" it might have saved me some uncomfortable afternoons at the movies.

Capra had and has his defenders, of course, but it seems to me that, as Chesterton said of Dickens, his reputation has suffered less from his enemies than from the enemies of his enemies. Their point always seemed to be that, after all, along with our usual diet of important, harsh, questioning films, there is room for soothing, pleasant, reassuring pictures like these. Capra is to be appreciated as a classic Hollywood entertainer—a manufacturer of slick, funny, technically brilliant crowd-pleasers. But if Capra is nothing more than an expert confectioner of highly effective but admittedly artificial "feel-good" movies, then his films are not merely unimportant but contemptible, because the joy and tears they stir up are produced by trifling with our deepest longings and most delicate hopes about courage, faith, God and our own ultimate meaning. There may be some point in saying that to show Jimmy Stewart goaded into committing suicide and rescued only by divine intervention is manipulative and melodramatic; there is at all none in calling the experience of watching it "soothing."

Just why these pictures inspire this stupendous polarity of opinions is a question I've struggled all my life to understand. I now believe that the answer is to be found within the very fabric of the theme being explored.

The Great Frank Capra Movie Mystery

If one had only Capra's reputation to go by, without knowing the man or seeing the films, I suppose that one might come to create a mental portrait of him as some smiling white-haired sentimentalist, perhaps a retired Congregationalist minister, with eyes full of easy tears and a fondness for quoting Norman Vincent Peale. In reality, Frank Capra was not only a hard-nosed, up-from-poverty immigrant with a rather acidic sense of humor (the biggest laughs in his films are cynical cracks from jaded sophisticates mocking the callow Capra hero), he was actually an intellectual –almost a rationalist. He was certainly every inch the Cal Tech Chemical Engineer of his school years. In fact, in Capra's unique background I've found what has been, for me, the whole key to the mystery of his films and their strange fate at the hands of the critics.

Frank Capra was raised a Catholic in a devout family of Sicilian peasants. He grew up watching these peasants live out a pathetic and backbreaking life of everyone working three jobs and going hungry anyway. The considerable happiness they found together in spite of these circumstances was largely sustained by their religious beliefs. Frank's father Salvatore also believed strongly in the old fable of "America as the land of opportunity." He died in a machine accident trying to improve their lot. Thus Capra was raised to believe in two ideals; democracy and the dignity of man—with the Christian Faith as the way to understand man and his destiny. Within this framework, he was encouraged to find the meaning of their humble lives and their very considerable troubles. Within this framework, Capra saw that his father, Salvatore Capra, though he was a dead, illiterate peasant buried in a hole, had been made in the image of God; he had mattered and still mattered.

In other words, Capra was raised a "true believer" and we can certainly find in this upbringing the origins of *It's A Wonderful Life* and what became known as "Capra-corn." Had these ideals never been challenged, he might well have gone on to become just the simple, faithful optimist he is so monotonously labeled. That is probably just what Frank Capra would have liked to have been; like Clarence the Angel—the simple, happy American untroubled by doubt. But his two ideals *were* challenged.

The young Frank Capra had another side. He wanted nothing more than an education; he saw it as his only way out of the peasant life of poverty he hated. He scratched and clawed his way into college and worked twenty hour days to stay there. Those eager to paint Capra as the Apostle of Easy Answers don't often see the need to draw attention to this thirst for knowledge and the hard won literacy and learning it brought him. Once in college, he studied not religion or poetry but chemistry—the science of what things are made of if you take them apart and boil them down. This sudden plunge into the world of natural science, this schooling in the scientific method in an atmosphere of skepticism and insistence on hard proof ensured that Capra would be denied the untroubled life of the "true believer." For the first time, he was presented with the possibility that Salvatore Capra was not an angel in heaven but a sack of bones in a box—so many grams of carbon and calcium. Of course, I don't mean to imply that all chemists are nihilists, but all chemists do deal, in their own various ways, with the specter of nihilism. They have all glanced into that pit and come up from their microscopes wondering, if only for a moment, whether it isn't all just a random arrangement of molecules after all and all their ideals just so much wishful thinking. Add this dose of rationalism to the street-wise persona he'd acquired as a short man growing up in the Italian ghetto (his first job offer as a Chemist, by the way, was the chance to make a quick killing designing stills for the mob), and you will get an idea of the forces that turned Capra into a skeptic. These things ensured that the cinema of Frank Capra would be the cinema, not of blind faith, but of doubt.

In fact, Frank Capra's skeptical outlook is so unmistakable that one can profitably consider the whole filmography of the scientist-turned-motion picture director as a series of scientific experiments. Out of his lifelong experience wrestling with this conflict in his heart, Capra has devised a series of demonstrations—demonstrations designed to present his hypothesis, apply his method of testing it, and produce his challenging result.

Far from finishing in that "happy-ending-land" of Mom and God and Norman Rockwell that he has been supposed to inhabit so blithely, Capra actually begins there. That world of family and democracy and human dignity is his *hypothesis*. Can it be believed? It is certainly warming and attractive but is it sound? Does it correspond to reality? We want to know. We need to know before we can be asked to stick our necks out for it. And so, faithful to his training, Capra the Chemist begins dispassionately and systematically turning up the Bunsen-burners of doubt, despair, and tragedy. He turns them up until that hypothesis is boiling in a beaker of betrayal and disillusionment so hot that the test simply cannot fail to uncover whether this "Capra-corn" he grew up believing can actually stand as a viable picture of the way things really are—or whether it will be revealed to have been, as Copernicus revealed the Ptolomeic cosmology to have been, nothing but a comforting fantasy.

This does not, of course, mean that Capra is suggesting that there really is any such town as archetypically perfect as Bedford Falls or that the whole world is full of John Does and Jeff Smiths. He has isolated the qualities he seeks to examine and presents them in their chemical purity. His cast of characters always falls into two simple and elemental categories—the idealists and the cynics. The idealists are the salt of the earth and the cynics are the acid. The Chemist exposes the two substances to each other: Mr. Deeds goes to town, Mr. Smith goes to Washington. And then Capra stands back and records the explosive result.

Our curiosity to see how the experiment will turn out is the engine that drives these stories along so compellingly. What will happen to Peter Warne, the newspaper poet, now that he's stuck his neck out to love a runaway heiress—and she has taken him for "a buggy ride with all the trimmings?" What will billionaire munitions magnate A. P. Kirby do now that his heartless maneuverings have killed and old friend—a friend who died with the warning "you can't take it with you" on his lips? What will Longfellow Deeds do when he finds out that "Mary Dawson" his "lovely angel" is actually wisecracking ace reporter "Babe" Bennett who has been making love to him for a month's vacation with pay? And what will *she* do when he finds out? You see, we are just as interested in Capra's hypothesis as he is... and just as dubious.

Running the Capra Gauntlet

Indeed, one of the most effective (and amusing) aspects of Capra's films is the way in which Capra the Cynic narrates (and really mocks and resists) a fairy tale dreamed up by Capra the Optimist. Thus Capra's films are full of cynics like himself: Saunders in *Mr. Smith*, The Colonel in *Meet John Doe*, Cornelius Cobb in *Mr. Deeds* (who even bears a strong physical resemblance to Capra). These cynics are Capra's stand-ins. We experience the story through their eyes—through the eyes of doubt. In this way, Capra gives expression to that part of himself (and that part of us) which is afraid of being taken in, the part that is just as embarrassed by these proceedings as his most red-faced critic. We are encouraged to laugh at the impossibly idealistic hero—Mr. Smith brings pigeons "to send messages home to Maw;" Mr. Deeds plays his tuba and chases fire engines. But then, as we see the storm clouds gathering over his head, this Capra hero begins to worry us a little. The sap has brought it on himself, of course, for going out so far on his creaky limb, but we like him and don't want to see him get hurt. He's a little lost puppy about to be run over by a very big truck. "Go home!" says Saunders, on a Smith-inspired drunk. "Get out of here! Stop hanging around making people feel sorry for you." Then the Capra hero starts to make us angry: we see very clearly now that this person has somehow managed to stay pure and that we sold out a very long time ago. So we laugh at him some more, but most of the fun has gone out of it now. Finally, we have mocked the Capra hero until he hangs bleeding from his cross. And then we get to step back and have a good look at what we've done.

As we noticed of George Bailey earlier, these Capra heroes could have gotten off this funeral train at any time; their high ideals have brought them nothing but the defeat we foresaw from the beginning. But somehow we don't feel like saying, "I told you so." We have become morbidly fascinated. This hero has courted the worst of the chaotic forces that hammer our dreams into the ground. He has challenged them to single-combat, as it were. This fool has positively dared them to come out and prove to us what we've always feared most; that our ideals are just wishful thinking, self-maintained fantasies that we cherish in order to keep our sanity. But now that he's done it we're eager to watch the scene play out. The hero's life, dedicated to Capra's twin pillars of faith and human dignity, is to be tested in the chemist's furnace because we need to know the truth—we need to know whether that life or any life so conceived and so dedicated can long endure.

And so, as we watch these martyrdoms, we come to the essence of Frank Capra's message: These things have been exhaustively tested, tried, fired in the crucible. I –Capra the Scientist, Capra the Skeptic—have tested them for you in my cinematic laboratory.

I have mocked the gentle Vermont poet Longfellow Deeds until he could do nothing but mutely suffer, silent like a sheep before its shearers, while his "lady-in-distress" made him such a laughingstock that they finally railroaded him off to an insane asylum.

I took Robert Conway, the world-weary dreamer, to the top of the world where, in the Valley of the Blue Moon, I raised his hopes so high that when I finally yanked the Tibetan rug from under his feet he fell so far and so hard he vowed never to get up again.

I tricked a hobo named Long John Willoughby into believing he was somebody and had something to say and then I pelted him with rotten fruit for saying it. Then I drove him back out into the hobo jungles where I have him his choice between jumping off a skyscraper roof on Christmas Eve or going insane.

I sent young Jefferson smith, the Boy Ranger who "can tell you what Washington and Jefferson said…by heart!" to the U.S. Senate where I had him jeered at, lied about, unjustly condemned and betrayed by those whom he most admired. I slapped him down every time he raised his head and spat on him until even his friends begged him to give up his lost cause and I left him looking up at an empty sky and silently crying out "My God, my God! Why hast thou forsaken me?"

And most of all, I made a visionary and a genius and named him George Bailey. I gave him a roaring wanderlust and set his heart aching for the stars. And then I put him in that hick town and never let him out and I never will.

I did all these things. Then I, Capra the Doubting Thomas, stood back to record what would happen…

Deeds, going down for the last time with his faith gone, was caught and rescued by city slickers on the way up, city slickers in whom he had created faith without knowing it.

Conway saw with his own eyes the infallible proof that turned him back to Shangri-La and transformed him into a raging superman who turned all Asia upside-down.

John Doe, the aimless drifter who had cared for nothing but baseball, found within himself the strength to fling his life away for the people who had rejected him and they, in turn, found in his sacrifice the strength to believe when belief is so very, very hard.

Jeff Smith never gave up his lost cause. Jeff was saved because his enemy finally threw up his hands and was converted, his towering fortress of cynicism breached by the inescapable proof of Jeff's words.

And George Bailey was sent the miracle for which so many, many people were praying that snowy Christmas Eve.

And having seen all these things, I record my testimony. This is my witness; this is the good news—the Gospel According to Frank Capra. These heroes bet their lives on what they believed...and what they believed was true. And now I now and am persuaded that their faith was not in vain. This is a true saying and worthy of all men to be received. It's A Wonderful Life.

Avant-Garde Cinema

This is why Frank Capra, contrary to popular opinion, is one of the most challenging of all filmmakers and in some ways the most disturbing. Most "serious films"—the "hard-hitting" "uncompromising" films—ask us only to accept, for example, that poverty is bad, relationships are hard, that politics is corrupt. In short, their "challenge" consists precisely in asking us to accept ideas that we already accept anyway, even if we struggle to know just what to do about them. In these comedies, Capra asks us to accept that the old-fashioned American ideals are still good, that David really can whip Goliath, that our prayers do not go unheard, that the meek shall inherit the earth. In other words, he asks us to accept things about which we have grave, grave doubts. And he is uncompromising in his asking: he doesn't ask us to accept these propositions as nice or inspirational or comforting or helpful—he asks us to accept them as true. That, my friend, is a challenging filmmaker. That is serious, avant-garde cinema, if you will.

Not many years ago, I was directed by a friend to another traditional Christmas movie, the 1948 comedy *Miracle on 34th Street*, starring Maureen O'Hara and young Natalie Wood: "You'll like it" he said "It's very Capra-esque." I appreciated the tip, but after watching the film I had to tell him that it was not Capra-esque at all. In fact, I had to tell him that *Miracle on 34th Street* is the exact and precise opposite of *It's A Wonderful Life*. The contrast between these two films has helped me to understand the uniqueness of Capra's challenge ever since.

Miracle on 34th Street is about a charming old fellow named Kris Kringle (marvelously played, by the way, by veteran Edmund Gwenn), who works as a holiday Santa Claus at Macy's Department Store. Trouble is, he claims there really is a true Santa Claus and he's it. Some people believe him and some don't; Maureen is inclined to have faith and little Natalie decidedly is not. The whole cast (idealists and cynics) spends the entire running-time of the picture attempting to prove or disprove Kris Kringle's claims. There's even a trial in a court-of-law, not unlike Mr. Deed's sanity hearing. Sounds just like a Capra movie, doesn't it? Actually, no. *Miracle on 34th Street* never does tell us whether the old chap really is Father Christmas himself or just a jolly old nut. In fact, the film makes rather a point of denying us this information. *Miracle* makes a point of saying that it doesn't matter whether Santa Claus really exists or not. What matters is that, if we all got together and decided to believe in Santa (whether he's real or not), the world would be much happier and sunnier and we'd treat each other better and I dare say we would. But Frank Capra is a hard-headed, unsentimental realist. He'd rather know the truth than be happy and sunny. The Capra hero has already seen *Miracle on 34th Street*; when the curtain rises on a Capra hero, he is already the sort of person who believes in Santa. George Bailey is a Santa Claus man from way back. But it isn't enough. With a cruel realism, Capra knows that our hero must be handed over to sinful men and crucified if we are to know whether his cherished beliefs are worthy of him. If Santa Claus is a myth then our faith is in vain. If George Bailey's guardian angel hadn't jumped into that river to save him, George would have drowned himself in it; and we are not encouraged to accept that believing in Clarence whether he is real or not would have done just as well.

And *there* is the whole difference between these two classic Christmas movies...between these two universes. *Miracle on 34th Street* is polite. It tactfully lets us off the hook. Because of this, many critics see it as by far the more sophisticated—the more "mature"—of the two; just because your father fell down dead and worms ate him is no reason to lose your sunny disposition. But Capra is rude. He presses us on the point. Either be a cynic or be an idealist if you can, but don't be an idealistic cynic. Either rage away at the idiot forces that obliterated your father or go and listen—really listen –to the case for Democracy, Dignity, and Faith and see if you can believe it.

The essence of Capra's unique challenge is his claim to have made that choice and come away from that search convinced that the case for these things really can be believed...that there are good and sufficient reasons for maintaining that it's a wonderful life. I think this is the reason his films are dismissed with derision by so many critics. Capra believes he has faced his doubts and been true to his doubts by wrestling with them honestly until the doubts were resolved. It's that resolution that puts him out of step with the modern mind. His claim to be satisfied—to have looked for answers and gotten them—invalidates Capra's message for those who disbelieve that such certainty ever comes. When one has decided from the outset that there are no ultimate answers to be had, Capra's vision can only seem grotesque and mawkish. Capra's films require a more open mind. If a person has made up his mind that there are no answers, then any answers at all are easy answers, even those purchased with the blood of martyrs.

But now that I think of it, probably most viewers of *It's A Wonderful Life* and these other Capra movies don't have such doctrinaire objections to what they see. After all, if Frank Capra sides with Socrates, Aquinas, Descartes, and Pascal (not to mention Shakespeare, Lao Tse, and T.S. Eliot) in daring to suggest that there are answers—glorious answers—to man's questions, than surely his reasons for adopting this philosophy are not subjects completely unworthy of treatment on film. Probably most of the people who are skeptical about *It's A Wonderful Life* actually *like* the film—even love it deep down inside—or wish they could; at any rate, they have the good sense to be troubled by it. I suspect that many of these folks might express their feelings by saying that Capra's picture of the universe is simply too good to be true. God bless them, I don't half blame them myself sometimes. Perhaps they know why they are so convinced of this and perhaps they don't but certainly they know the stakes involved. Capra calls us to stick our necks out and that call is so very frightening. He is offering us a ticket into the world we would all most like to believe in—a world where every person matters and where no one is alone—but the price of admission is commitment. Capra is wooing us and, like shy country brides, we are afraid of him. Every instinct in modern man urges us to hedge our bets. "Remember," we tell ourselves, "if you don't expect much from life, nothing can hurt you very much." And this is very true and very sensible. But if we take this attitude we will also have prevented life from being very wonderful. It may be still manage to be comfortable, safe, even pleasant—but it can never be truly wonderful in the deepest, most ancient and "Capra-esque" sense of that word. In order to prevent the world from bursting our beautiful balloon, we will have taken our own needles and burst it ourselves. If we cling to this frame of mind—if we refuse the call to stick our necks out for something—Capra's wholesome, healing vision will only cause us pain; his sweet songs will only torment us and we will have to stop listening.

Weathering the Storm

Let me urge you rather to listen to Capra. Listen to him with wide open eyes and wide open hearts if you can. Pretend you are an unhappy, ignorant fourteen-year-old on two weeks Christmas vacation, if it seems to help. The next time *It's A Wonderful Life* comes on TV watch it and try to imagine, if only for 129 minutes, that it hasn't been conclusively proven to be nothing but "a simple figment of Pollyanna platitudes." Pretend for a little while that you don't know as an established fact that this world of dignity, destiny, and guardian angels is too good to be true. After all, what can it hurt to try Capra's faith on for size for an hour or two, just to see how it feels? Because Capra insists that if we will give him a chance he will prove his case.

Yes, it's true that if we hitch our wagon to George Bailey's star we will be crucified with him and buried under $8,000 worth of bitter defeat. But the director insists that if we are crucified with him then we will be raised with him. If we share in the Capra hero's dark night of the soul, we will be rescued by hard evidence and the fruit that will have sprung up from the seeds of faith he has planted. George's $8,000 defeat will be swallowed up in Bedford Falls' avalanche of victory poured into that old hat passed around in his drafty old house on Christmas Eve -- and by a telegram from London…

HEARD YOU WERE IN TROUBLE -- STOP -- MY OFFICE INSTRUCTED TO ADVANCE YOU UP TO $25,000 -- STOP -- HEE HAW AND MERRY CHRISTMAS. SAM WAINWRIGHT.

Yes, George Bailey, there is a Santa Claus. You have proved it to us now. You were right. You were right all along. It *is* a wonderful life. You have weathered the storm and we who went along for the ride have been taught the Gospel..."To him that overcometh I will give to eat of the tree of life, which is in the midst of the paradise of God."

Now, only now, can we have our happy ending, perhaps the happiest in Hollywood history.

Originally published in *Gadfly Magazine*, December 1997

A MORE CIVILIZED AGE: THE DISTURBING FAITH OF GEORGE LUCAS

Not too long ago, in a galaxy called the 1970s, a skinny film school graduate in jeans and sneakers got together with a bunch of hippies, sci-fi nerds and other counter-cultural types, and tinkered together a movie that almost single-handedly rescued cinema for his generation. This spring, George Lucas is back and, believe it or not, he still wants to know if his jerry-rigged update of *Flash Gordon* can make you smile. Yes, folks, the big movie release for the spring of 1997 figures to be a little oddity called *Star Wars*.

This latter-day visitation by Luke Skywalker, Darth Vader, Princess Leia and kin—a $10 million restoration featuring gussied-up special effects and a state of the art THX soundtrack—may or may not recapture America's imagination. It seems sure, however, to reopen an old debate among Christians: what religious ideas, if any, is Star Wars propagating—and is this propagation a good thing or a bad thing?

Like any influential cultural phenomenon, the *Star Wars* trilogy has received its share of scrutiny, a good deal of it (at least from the Christian churches) of a negative or suspicious nature. Impressionistic youngsters, after all, get very excited about *Star Wars*—a good deal more excited, as a matter of fact, than they currently seem to be about reading the Bible or going to church. One might even say that Luke Skywalker had been the 1970s equivalent of John Lennon and the Beatles—more popular than Jesus Christ—and the message of *Star Wars* was much more overtly religious in nature than any Beatles song.

It's called "the Force" in the films; that dreamy pop Buddhism preached by Obi-Wan Kenobi and his muppet mentor Yoda. More than one concerned youth minister saw this element of the story as a sly form of

Eastern religious propaganda and a New Age plot—the second coming of the Maharishi Yoga. A bit of scratching into Mr. Lucas' own philosophical ponderings seemed only to confirm their misgivings; he admits to being strongly influenced by the writings of Carlos Casteneda, Hermann Hesse, and myth-meister Joseph Campbell, new age icons all. The films themselves are filled with such obscure religious wisdom as, "You must unlearn what you have learned," and "Why? There is no why!...Clear your mind of questions." This undeniably Eastern-flavored element is there in Star Wars for anyone to see—so obvious, in fact, that they may, it seems to me, have blinded many Christian critics to some equally apparent elements from their own tradition.

Many of these "Eastern plot" criticisms were, I believe, nothing but red herrings from the start. The fact, for instance, that "the Force" has a good side and a dark side has been taken to show that Mr. Lucas believes God has both good and evil within Him and that neither, therefore, must be suppressed in our own lives. Yet the films themselves never identify the Force with God at all. It's actually referred to as "a mystical energy field" which "binds us and penetrates us." "Life creates it," we are told, rather than the other way round, and "makes it grow." The Force, in other words, is not God but simply spiritual power—what atheists call ESP and what Evangelical writer Watchman Nee referred to as "the latent power of the soul."

The main thing, however, that has been overlooked in such criticism is the actual role played by "the Force" in the dynamics of the story. The "way of the Force" is never contrasted with or presented as an attractive alternative to the Judeo-Christian tradition; the story, recall, takes place "a long time ago in a galaxy far, far away." Lucas' writers have said that the so-called "religion of *Star Wars*" is nothing but their own vague speculation about the form religion might take in some remote corner of the universe which has never had any communication at all with our own. This religion is contrasted with the instantly recognizable atheistic materialism of the evil Galactic Empire. It's no coincidence that this evil empire of Star Wars looks and sounds so much like that distinctively mid-century historical nightmare: the modern, all-powerful secular State.

Recall this exchange between Darth Vader (though fallen from grace, still an apostle of the Force) and one of the Death Star's machine age bureaucrats…

General Tagge: Don't try to frighten us with your sorcerer's ways, Lord Vader. Your sad devotion to that ancient religion has not help you to conjure up the stolen data tapes…

Vader (taking a telekinetic choke hold on Tagge's throat): I find your lack of faith disturbing.

This plot device runs throughout the *Star Wars* trilogy: devotees of the

Force, even when on the outs with the good side, inhabit a world of knights and princesses and desert mystics, and stand in contrast to a lamentable "new order" of scientism and disbelief. Clearly, "the Force" stands less as a symbol for any one particular religion and more as a reverent evocation of "a more civilized age," of vanishing Religious Man, of a lost world-view of human significance and dignity which most of the world's major religions share—contrasted with modern meaninglessness, absurdity, and state manipulation.

Even so, it is significant that in creating their fantasy faith to do battle with secularism, Lucas and his compadres looked chiefly to the East for inspiration instead of to the civilization that actually created the concepts of knighthood and chivalry. Why? Because for Lucas' generation, I think, much of the glory of Western belief had departed. When every night the TV newscasts showed ostensibly Christian leaders willing to evoke the Bible in justification of segregation or of carpet bombing during the Vietnam war, many of the customary doors for religious expression seemed to be closing in their faces. Many Sixties-era young people, in fact, pursued Eastern religion because it was the only religion left for them—oddly enough, many of them pursued it as an alternative to the *atheism* toward which bad Christian witness was providing so much apparent justification.

Nevertheless, what really ought to be noted is how quickly the vagueness and non-committal nature of Eastern faith vanishes when the grand climax arrives. In *Return of the Jedi* (a decidedly *Western* story, by the way, about a son who risks his own life to prevent his errant father from dying with unrepented sin still on his soul), we find that a number of Lucas' characters are to lose their lives in the climactic throes of the struggle between good side and dark. And notice that when the issues are life and death, heaven and hell, time and eternity, Lucas and company show their true colors. Remember, if you will, that Jedi's happy ending includes a shot of our departed heroes (Ben Kenobi, Yoda, and Anakin Skywalker) looking on as those left behind celebrate their triumph—looking on, mind you, in recognizable bodily form, a concept anathema to all thoroughgoing Eastern religion, in which the ultimate victory is the loss of individuality, and death is "the slipping of a drop of water back into an endless ocean." But Lucas doesn't want those he loves slipping into any endless oceans. When facing the dark destroyer, George Lucas, like most Western men who play at what Chesterton called "the exalted apathy of the East," retreats back into the comfort of Judeo-Christian thought forms—"the communion of the saints, the forgiveness of sins, the resurrection of the dead, and the life everlasting."

Originally published in *Rutherford Magazine,* February 1997

MYSTERY IN THE WAX MUSEUM

Not so very long ago, back when I was a fundamentalist, two uneducated Tennessee mountaineers taught me the Catholic doctrine of the Veneration of Saints.

The first of these encounters happened when I was ten years old. My parents took me to the Smoky Mountain resort town of Gatlinburg, famous in 17 states for caramel apples, Elvis shrines, haunted houses, and, best of all, wax museums. One of these museums was a bit out of the ordinary, and my favorite. It was called *The American Historical Wax Museum*; a quaint, immaculately tidy little "Mom & Pop" operation snuggled into a faux-colonial façade along the city's main drag. Mom & Pop were quite real, by the way, though I've long since forgotten their names. Mom was a seamstress, who made many of the costumes used in the exhibit herself. Pop was a decorated veteran of WWII—with the vibrant, living faith of mid-century Americanism coursing through his veins like sanctifying grace.

One didn't get the impression that his museum netted Pop much profit; it was more in the nature of a private devotion apparently. Contrary to standard wax museum practice, for instance, there wasn't a single figure of Marilyn Monroe or Charles Manson in the place. Instead, its hallowed halls echoed with the angelic sounds of a hushed choir, singing "Red River Valley," "The Battle Hymn of the Republic" or "Shenandoah." And instead of movie stars or mass murderers, the carefully lighted wax tableaux featured scenes like "Washington Crossing the Delaware" and "Lee Surrenders to Grant at Appomattox Court House." In response, as I recall, the public stayed away in droves; but Mom & Pop seemed to count it all joy.

In particular, it was the climactic scene here that affected me for life.

Visitors were ushered solemnly into a "Hall of Tennessee Heroes." After filing respectfully past wax statues of people like Andrew Jackson, Cordell Hull, and James K. Polk, you ultimately entered a large dimly lit theatre that slowly came to life through the use of dramatic theatrical lighting and piped-in music. Before long, you saw that the scene being depicted was the death of the greatest local hero of them all, Davy Crockett, at the hands of Santa Ana's army in the battle of the Alamo, 1836. Sprawled backward over the barricades, clutching the flag of Texas independence in one hand, his buckskin outfit splashed with blood, Davy is magnificent in defeat. A Mexican soldier is in the very act of piercing his breast with a cold bayonet; a soft radiance falls on his face from above like a halo. His eyes, lifted up to heaven in an ecstasy of resignation, are eloquent with their unspoken message: "Father, into Thy hands I commend my spirit." Though I knew nothing of this at the time, it was a scene straight out of what is commonly called "bad Catholic art." Just as corny, just as overwrought, just as sublime. And just as capable of wrenching sensitive little boys onto strange, unpredictable paths in life.

The second of these rather unconventional lessons in human sanctity happened a few years later, when I first discovered (and fell in love with) Howard Hawks' 1941 movie classic *Sergeant York*. Alvin C. York, as you may remember, was the true-life American hero of World War I and a Congressional Medal of Honor recipient. Born in the remote valley of the three forks of the Wolf River, near Pall Mall, Tennessee, Alvin (played by Gary Cooper in the film) entered adulthood in the 1910's as a hard-working, hard-drinking, two-fisted mountain wild man. Sentenced by fate to his culture's underclass (who, ironically, live on the top—on the worthless rocky hillsides left over when the gentry claimed the fertile valleys below) Alvin wrestles with God as Jacob wrestled with the angel. Resisting the witness of the village parson (Walter Brennan), ignoring the prayers and entreaties of his saintly mother (Margaret Wycherly), York will pay Jehovah back for His unfairness by making a success of himself *without* divine help, by sheer backbreaking human effort. We watch as he comes tantalizingly close, within sight of his goal, and then, at the last moment, is swindled out of his place in the sun by one of the very bottomlanders he so bitterly envies.

The next scene is dark, apocalyptic, with all the horror and human realism of an Old Testament Bible story. Alvin has murder in his eyes as he drinks himself to the point of violent action. Nothing his friends can do or say will stop him; he shakes them off and strides out into a howling storm, intent on bloody vengeance — and his own damnation. Yet halfway down this road to Damascus there is a flash of blinding light and the peal of thunder. A bolt of lightning blasts his dripping mule off its feet, sends Alvin himself flying into the mud, deaf with the voice of God. When he can think again, he rises, looks around, and finds his rifle—the instrument he would have used to slay his brother—lying red hot on the ground, twisted and curled like one of Uri Geller's spoons.

Now, instead of hunting down his victim Alvin stumbles through the rain to the nearby church, where an evening prayer meeting is in session. He enters, hat in hand, and kneels repentant at the altar, before the congregation and before God, with the lightning still crackling across the firmament. His mother looks on in speechless wonder, then lifts her hands heavenward in wordless praise — the hillbilly reincarnation of St. Monica. The whole assembly erupts into rejoicing; Brennan's wild-eyed Pastor Pyle calls for a new hymn, *That Old Time Religion* — the closest fundamentalism ever gets to a litany of the saints:

"It was good for the prophet Dan'l…
"It was tried in the fiery furnace…
"It was good for Paul and Silas…
"It's good enough for me."

You couldn't help but think that the name of Alvin C. York himself had now been added that litany—I certainly did, at any rate, though what little I knew of Catholicism I hated.

At this point in the story the parallels to St. Augustine become even more trenchant, for York becomes a Bible teacher, an ardent lover of Christ, and, in his own homespun way, something of a Christian philosopher. With the advent of the draft in 1918 we watch him wrestle valiantly with the age-old problems of Christian pacifism, non-resistance, and the concept of a "just war."

Finally, after triumphing gloriously over his enemies, both literal and metaphorical, the humble, hallowed Alvin C. York receives his Medal of Honor. And the scene plays like a *coronation* — no, like a beatification. Yes, I watched the movie as a convinced Southern Baptist, committed to the proposition that any veneration offered to a mere human was the rankest blasphemy. And yet I couldn't help myself. As the wreath was lowered onto Sgt. York's shoulders I heard (and still hear whenever I watch it) a silent voice from above:

"Well done, thou good and faithful servant: thou hast been faithful over a few things, I will make thee ruler over many things: enter thou into the joy of thy Lord."

It sounds silly, I suppose, getting so worked up about a cheesy wax museum and a corny black & white movie. But for me, these things were like signal flares in the night, offering brief glimpses into an unexplored world of religious emotion that my current faith simply wasn't addressing at all.

Later, when I was old enough to drive, I made a secret pilgrimage to Sgt. York's burial place. Though still an anti-Catholic Evangelical, something seemed to compel me; on a hot summer day in the mid-1980s I got into my car alone and made the long trip up to Pall Mall, Tennessee. And when I did, I found that not even the United States Government could restrain itself: the resting place of Sgt. York's relics is now marked with *an eternal flame*; the inchoate prayer of a spiritually stunted people, the votive light of a nation whose hearts are purer than their philosophy.

Today, as a full-fledged, saint-invoking, Romanist "idolater," I understand what it is that was happening to me back then. The saints (even ersatz saints like these) mirror, in ways that nothing else can, the One who is the source of all sanctity, the fountain of all holiness. Yes, it's true, in one sense, that God alone is worthy of praise, and He's jealous of His worship and willing to share it with no one. But God wants to be worshipped *in* something, *for* something—in the power of His might and for the works of His mighty Hand.

Alvin York, for example, had been quite a project, and I think God is rather proud of what He accomplished in that particular case. He wants *us* to see that, too, and to praise Him for His artistry; just as He wants to be praised for the masterpiece that is the Moon, for the Pleiades and Orion. And even in the death of Davy Crockett (whose true-life exploits my mature judgment now holds far more suspect than York's) I had seen God's glory in the beauty of *martyrdom*, in the willingness to surrender one's own life that some other created thing might live.

As an Evangelical I had been told that God alone is holy, that His holiness is, in the words of a prominent Protestant theologian, "an incommunicable attribute." But the joyful Catholic truth is just the opposite. God is striving every day, through the agency of His Holy Spirit, to make us all *truly holy*—and by golly, sometimes He succeeds! Thus the saints become the perfect mirror of God's own excellence.

There is one last point I'd like to make about this mystery found in the wax museum. It's a rather sad one, I'm afraid, and a point I regret to bring forward. But the truth is that I *still* have to go to the wax museum to experience this particular mystery. The Catholic churches in my diocese have, for the most part, been stripped of all their saints, and without any Henry VIII to blame for the outrage. Those few that remain have been rendered abstractly, in an inhuman, aggressively symbolic style. And most of the church buildings they decorate could easily pass for the Protestant Pavilion at the 1964 New York World's Fair.

Don't get me wrong. I do think that Catholic art should be good art. When the saints do finally go marching back into our churches, let them be rendered with skill, with subtlety, and with good taste. But let them not forget to speak to the *heart*, about primary things like virtue, heroism, self-sacrifice — the things a ten-year old understands. For unless we all become like little children again we will in no wise see the kingdom of God.

At any rate, as soon as I finish this essay I'm leaving for the weekend on a trip back up to Gatlinburg. I think I will take some candles and incense with me.

And I'll pray in the wax museum until the manager calls the cops.

Originally published by *Catholic Exchange*, Summer 2001

GOING TO BAT FOR *SONG OF THE SOUTH*

I own a copy of a banned motion picture. I showed it to my wife and young son the other night. They agreed with me; censorship is bad...but it sure is fun to watch something that no one else on your street is allowed to see.

The movie in question is Walt Disney's 1946 release *Song of the South*, starring James Baskett, Hattie McDaniel, and Ruth Warwick. Based on the famous African-American folk tales collected by journalist Joel Chandler Harris as the *Uncle Remus Stories*, *Song of the South* surrounds stunning animated adaptations of them with a live-action "picture frame"; a sincerely felt parable in which the ancient wisdom contained in an old slaves fireside yarns builds a bridge between husband and wife, between black and white. Once a cherished part of America's cultural legacy, these stories are much less well-known today than they ever have been; the same misguided forces that are currently conspiring to keep this film out of your hands have attached a thoroughly undeserved stigma to one of the world's great literary treasures...a treasure, in fact, which all Americans share together. And the film is one of Disney's best. The live portions are tenderly sketched (and feature some of the most luminous Technicolor ever shot—by the legendary Gregg Toland), and the animated episodes rank with the finest work the studio ever produced. That this wonderful movie is so difficult to see today is simply a crime.

The 1940s were, on the whole, a terrible dry spell for Disney. The high-brow critics who had feted and championed Walt's work in the 30s turned their backs on him after *Fantasia* and the driving spirit of innovation which had characterized the pre-war years dried up amidst bitter labor disputes and hard times brought on by the loss of the lucrative overseas markets. The animated short subject in particular lost all of the luster audiences had come to expect from watching the elaborate Mickey Mouse films and highly experimental *Silly Symphonies* of the previous decade. The live-action arm of the studio (which in the 1950s would add new stars to Walt's crown with such classics as *Twenty Thousand Leagues Under the Sea, Darby O'Gill and the Little People,* and the remarkable *True-Life Adventures* nature series) was only just being born—at first, a mere expediency brought on by a wartime British law which decreed that profits from American films shown in England must be spent in England. But *Song of the South* is a true classic. Three of the original Uncle Remus tales—"The Briar Patch", "The Tar Baby", and "Brer Rabbit's Laughing Place"—come to life with unprecedented vividness. About these segments, Disney historian Leonard Maltin has written, "They have a joy, a cheerfulness about them that is absolutely irresistible and, of course, they are populated with delightful songs, such as the Academy Award winner *Zip-A-Dee-Doo-Dah* and *Everybody's Got A Laughin' Place*…(This film) perfected the combination of animation and live-action to a height of perfection…" Indeed, *Song of the South* seems an almost ideal use of the animation medium, and it looks doubly impressive when compared with roughly contemporary Disney efforts like *Saludos Amigos*, *Fun and Fancy Free*, and *Melody Time*.

Unfortunately, *Song of the South*—a lovely, charming little picture without a mean bone in its body—somehow, in the last twenty years or so, managed to get itself onto somebody's ideological *hit list. It was last given a tentative, timid theatrical release in 1986—whereupon on or two highly unbalanced op-ed pieces from extremist sources caused the studio to rush out an apology and promise never to do it again. And the Disney Company has been as good as its word: the picture has not been seen or heard from since. It is conspicuously absent from Walt Disney Home Video's massively profitable VHS line-up and is never shown on television. *Song of the South* has been thoroughly suppressed—vanished down the memory hole like a bad book in Stalinist Russia. The contraband copy with which I polluted my family is an expensive laserdisc imported from Japan.

Exactly who is it that hates *Song of the South* so badly? I confess I'm at a loss. The only group I can think of that might have some semi-rational cause for doing so is the Ku Klux Klan. I do remember coming out of the theatre so awed at James Baskett's wonderful performance (he not only plays Uncle Remus but voices about a dozen other characters as well) that I walked all the way to the car wishing I wasn't so bland and, well…white. Yes, I, a lilywhite Southerner found myself mourning the fact that I can't sound natural calling little kids "honeychile" and can't think up philosophy as profound as "You cain't run away from trouble, Honey…they ain't no place dat fur." And this, from the KKK's point of view, is obviously a deeply perverse and unnatural occurrence. Yes, that must be it; some people are so wicked that they simply can't tolerate any film in which blacks are portrayed in such a heroic light.

Because make no mistake—Uncle Remus certainly is the hero of *Song of the South*. In fact, he's the only really sympathetic character in the film over the age of seven and without fur. Ruth Warwick (Citizen Charles Foster Kane's first wife in Welle's classic five years previous) played so many icy, repressed harridans in her first few years in Hollywood that she eventually stopped getting parts and had to retire from pictures. Her plantation mistress here is another, and it seems completely impossible that anyone should consider her Remus' superior in any way. Her husband (played by Eric Rolf)—who is ostensibly lord and master of this realm—is, in fact, the most passive character in the picture. He abandons his wife and family for a political career in Atlanta and only reclaims them after a dose of Uncle Remus' wisdom. Slave he may be, but nothing could be clearer than that Uncle Remus is possibly freer and certainly wiser and happier than his on-paper master and mistress. In fact, this seems to be the point of the film. Song of the South goes to great lengths to contrast the strain and tension of life in the "big house" with the spiritual health, vitality, and interconnectedness of Remus' community. The white folks have political freedom, to be sure: they use it to spin intricate webs of self-made bondage. Remus is a slave—and spends his time merely serving as prophet, grandfather, priest, and counselor to everyone on the plantation, black or white.

This is not to say that Remus is happier as a slave than he would be free, nor that his political emancipation is a matter of irrelevance; merely that political freedom is not the only type of freedom.

In all seriousness, I actually think that this is the point where the people who take umbrage here go astray. I believe that their trouble with *Song of the South* may lie precisely with Uncle Remus' obvious *happiness*—the happiness itself is offensive. To them, this picture is obviously just another example of that old guilt-assuaging Southern fantasy wherein the "happy darkies" actually did nothing all day but sit on the magnolia-lined banks of the Suwanee strummin' on the ol' banjo. Apparently, for a film to show an African slave in the antebellum South in any attitudes other than abject misery or seething rebellion is to suggest that the "peculiar institution" wasn't as bad as it has been painted or that slavery was really tolerable after all. In reality, *Song of the South* does show, in its gentle way, that Uncle Remus is often treated badly. His word is often doubted for no other reason than his color, and when unhappy little Johnny innocently suggests that the two of them should run away from home together, Remus' poignant awareness of his bondage is heartbreaking. But to insist that black slaves may only be depicted either (1) writhing under the whip, or (2) stealing guns with John Brown, is to miss the whole meaning of freedom. Even if archaeology were to suddenly prove (this is certainly not the case) that the actual conditions of slavery were tranquil and pleasant—a life spent rocking on the veranda and sharing a mint julep with the Colonel—the issue would still be the same: the institution of slavery itself was immoral. For a man to own another man's body in the same way he owns a tool, like a hammer or shovel, is intrinsically evil—even if the man lets his "tool" become something like a favorite lap dog. The problem with slavery is most definitely *not* that the slave-owners treated their property badly (though that was often true). This issue is that they treated them as property at all. Take away every drop of blood drawn by the lash and the abolition of slavery was still worth every drop of blood drawn by the sword.

This is why Uncle Remus is actually such an ennobling figure for modern African-Americans—and indeed, for anyone whose ancestors were enslaved or oppressed (which is about 85% of all Americans). Uncle Remus represents the genius of Man in his ability to free his mind and spirit even if the body is still in chains. A vote may be an excellent thing but even before you get it, you have dignity—because you can dream up stories like "The Tar Baby." It is certain that Uncle Remus is not enjoying the political freedom which is his right as a man—but until then, he is certainly enjoying freedom of mind and spirit, to a greater degree than many of us who do vote (every now and then).

Now, I'm sure that at this point at least one well-meaning soul, in a spirit of liberality and open-mindedness, will rush in with this curious thought—"You see, this cracker thinks the blacks should have been content to sit by the fire and be quaint…and let their betters do the voting." To which I can only reply that by now, most of us—whatever color we may be—realize that if our meaning and self-worth were to depend entirely on political solutions (or worse, politicians) then we will never have meaning and self-worth. After all, in today's society, where injustice of every type rages about as hotly as ever, we can all take a lesson from a man who—if he predicts that his political emancipation will only be won after a struggle of, shall we say, twenty more years, refuses to put his happiness on hold until those twenty years are up. For Uncle Remus, at any rate, life was simply too precious. Even a slave has the blue infinity overhead, the spirit of God to catch him up to it, the love of family and friends, and the rabbit and fox for his brothers. They say that even the doomed at Auschwitz sang songs when a spring day was simply too warm and bright to resist. Yes, this does make their annihilation even more tragic—but it also makes their faces more human. They, like the Southern slaves, were not simply faceless sufferers, whose fates may be skillfully evoked as heavy rhetorical ammunition in a political argument. They were real living members of the family of Man—so full of life that even their "omnipotent" taskmasters failed to wring every last drop of happiness out of them.

The great G.K. Chesterton liked to point out that, even though liberators and emancipators are undoubtedly a good thing, they usually insist on bringing their own particular *brand* of liberation to those they free.

In contrast to this, Chesterton spoke of Joel Chandler Harris, who often referred to himself as "nothing but the mouthpiece for the humor, faith, and kindliness of the Negro."

"The ordinary northern idealist," wrote Chesterton, "preached generosity to the blacks, saying 'We will give the Negro light; we will give the Negro education.' Chandler Harris, in Uncle Remus, gave an indirect, unexpected, and yet strangely forcible answer. He did not say—'I will give the Negro whips and chains if he is mutinous,' or 'I will give him a better light and liberty if he is good.' No, he said—'This is what the Negro *has given me.* You talk of educating the slave; this is how the slave educated me. He taught me the primal culture of humanity, the ancient and elvish wisdom without which all other learning is priggishness, the tales which from the beginning our Mother Earth has told to all her children at night. The Negro has given something to the South…and I will give it to the North."

I hope that you will one day have an opportunity to see Walt Disney's *Song of the South* and give it a chance. As Uncle Remus himself put it, *"Dees tales ain't never done nobody no harm…and if dey don't do no good, why has dey lasted so long?"*

Originally published in *Wonder* #10, Spring 1995

ONE MAN'S PASSION: A TRAGICAL COMEDY IN THREE ACTS

Prologue: Summer 1982

This story properly begins with a television commercial.

It was Jacksonville, Florida's UHF independent, informing the world that on the very next balmy Saturday night they'd be showing Universal's 1935 classic *The Bride of Frankenstein*, a film which I've adored since I first saw it as a 12 year old.

I was in the Navy at the time, stationed at what was then the brand new submarine base at King's Bay—a majestic-sounding name for a very out of the way backwater spot on the picturesque Georgia coast. It was my duty-night, as I recall, and I was waiting up to stand the midnight watch, killing a little time in the crew's lounge watching TV. When that commercial came on it yanked me right out of my seat. It had been ten years since I'd seen *Bride* and ten years, at least, since it had played on TV in my hometown of Atlanta. And when I'd seen it in the early 70s, I certainly hadn't owned a VCR—nor had anyone. As the promo ended, I hastily took down the time and date of the showing—and noted with dismay that it happened to correspond with another upcoming duty night. But it didn't matter. I rashly resolved, then and there, not to miss taping that movie if they had to court-martial me for it.

It's probably difficult for young people to understand what a different world we movie buffs lived in during that long, hot summer—the summer President Reagan wrestled with a nasty little recession, the British fought a quick little war with Argentina, and a little movie called "E.T." became the biggest moneymaker in history. Those of us who love classic films like *The Bride of Frankenstein* are apt to forget just how good we've got it these days.

In 1982, less than 10% of homes had a VCR; many people didn't know what a VCR was for, and many of those who did couldn't see the point in owning one (especially when they looked at the price tag: a low-end model went for $500 plus). There simply wasn't that much to tape back then. The cable revolution was in its infancy; most Americans still got by on four or five broadcast channels, left under the tender care of the big three networks, who remained convinced that most of us were crazy about stuff like *The Love Boat* and *Fantasy Island.* For those who did have cable, HBO was all the rage. HBO showed three movies a day (immortals like *Cannonball Run* and *Porky's*) and repeated them about 40 times in one month. It is true that the very first video rental stores opened that year: I bought a membership at one that boasted 800 titles—one day rentals were $3.00 and the membership fee was 75 bucks! One could, if one chose, purchase a tape of one's favorite flick (provided one's favorite title was the latest new release)…for a mere $89.95. As far as access to the classics, I do recall that some friends and I were able to rent a Beta format tape of the original *King Kong* earlier that year. We saw an ad for it in a classy photography magazine and so we all pitched in and sent a check for $80 to New York City. In return, we were shipped a dark, murky tape of the edited version of the movie taken from a grainy 16mm print—and we thought we were in hog heaven. We were allowed to keep it for three whole days (we watched it several times) whereupon, if we returned it via UPS and it arrived in good condition, we got $60 of our money back. Like I said, it was a different world. I pause to evoke these pleasant memories only because I'm hoping they might help you understand why I was willing to go to some length to tape one of my childhood favorites.

No court-martial turned out to be necessary. I persuaded my Division Officer to juggle my schedule around—but still had to pay another sailor $20 to agree to work for me on the crucial Saturday night. Then I made a rush trip home to Atlanta to gather up my big Betamax unit. A six hour trip each way, in one 24-hour period, driving a beater I used to refer to as my "James Bond car"—a '78 Mustang that, when the accelerator was depressed, would deploy a smoke screen out the back and squirt oil all over the road. Roaring back into King's Bay the day before the movie was scheduled, I now had a tape deck and the day off—but there were still big plans to be made.

I couldn't use and of the TV sets at the Navy base; the fellers wouldn't understand (and the picture quality was usually lousy anyway). I decided to drive down to Jacksonville (about 40 miles south) where the station showing Bride was actually located, and thus get a really good recording. I'd check into a motel there, hook up to the set in the room, and nab my treasure in private. Maybe swim in the pool afterward to celebrate.

Well, Saturday came and I did pretty much just that. I found a motel not far from the beach—one of those turquoise-colored classic out of the 1960s, with names like *Sea Spray* or *Trade Winds*—checked in, stepped inside…and discovered that TV picture looked terrible. Just awful. Rushing out to a nearby Radio Shack, I bought an antenna of my own, and got it hooked up just in time for the start of the movie.

The film itself astounded me. It not only did it have all the wonderful Octobery feelings I remembered so well, it also had an intelligence and a panache that had been lost on a 12-year old. The technique was years ahead of its time and the script was full of a unique brand of black humor that I found (and still find) hilarious. It was very clear to me that I was watching one of the best films ever made and that all this trouble had been very, very worthwhile.

When the picture finished about 1AM, I rewound my new tape and watched nearly the whole thing again. Deciding that I was just pleased as punch about this whole little adventure, I finally turned off the lights about 3AM and got up the next day at the crack of lunch. Then I drove back to the Navy base with my prize, thoroughly satisfied with myself.

I was thoroughly *dissatisfied*, however, with the arrangements of the next week. I couldn't bring my VCR to work with me (living, as I did, aboard a Navy ship) so I was forced to leave it locked up in the trunk of the Mustang way back at the end of the pier. This being summertime in Georgia, I imagined that that trunk must be getting pretty cozy, if not downright oven-like. I really needed to find someplace else to store the recorder until I could find a weekend to take it back to Atlanta. This was easier said than done. As the days got hotter and hotter, I became more and more convinced that my $900 machine and cherish videotape were turning into useless goo. I got desperate.

I had a sometime-friend aboard ship named Wayland Welden—a slow-talking Alabamian about 7 feet tall with no visible sign of chin. He wasn't a bad guy, I guess, and had recently got married and brought his new wife down here to the swamps and marshes where she could live in crackerbox Navy housing ashore while he finished his stint. Anyhow, it occurred to me that Wayland and wife might let me store my unit there for a week or two until my schedule cleared up. I wasn't *entirely* confident in the guy, but how much harm could he do in just a few days?

I approached him with my plan and he readily agreed. So one afternoon when it was about 98 degrees outside, I took the machine (including the few videotapes I had brought with me, including the newly-minted *Bride*) over to his little stucco apartment. The place was brand new Navy housing, but cheap and kinda barren-looking sitting out there on the sand, with the sun beating down on it and the scrubby little pines poking up and armadillos crawling around everywhere. But I could hear an AC unit whirring someplace nearby and, yeah, once inside the little joint was dark and cool and so I gladly carried everything in. Wayland introduced me to his wife (I don't recall her actual name but she was a "Tammy" if I ever saw one). She led me to a spot she'd cleared off next to their modest little 19 inch set and I went ahead and set the unit up for them so that they could sample some of the wonders of the still-novel age of home video. They were very impressed. I suppose they thought of VCRs as something only rich people had—which was actually true for the most part in those days, excepting for big time movie nerds like myself. Anyway, it seemed only fair to let them watch the thing a little, seeing as how they were loaning me the space for free (and a VCR took up plenty back then, believe me). So I showed them how to turn it on, put in the tapes I'd loaned, etc. I did, at the same time however, give them some fairly stern instructions about *not* messing around with the *record* button; I remember that distinctly. Otherwise, I just thanked them for their hospitality, accepted a frosty glass of ice tea, and went back to the base.

About a week went by before I could go back and pick it up again. I'd arranged a weekend trip home and was all set to carry my delicate equipment out of harm's way at last. Liberty call Friday afternoon, and I was back over to the little sun-baked apartment to reclaim my machine on the way out of town. As it turns out, Wayland Welden had the duty that day, so it was his wife who opened the door. All smiles and howdies, she told me, nevertheless, that she was on the way to the grocery store and could I just take everything loose myself and pull the door to behind me? I reckoned that I could and so she left me there alone.

It was still early so, before getting to work, I thought I'd pop *Bride of Frankenstein* in for a minute or two and relive my triumph a little; after all, it'd been nearly two weeks since I'd acquired it. I found the tape, dropped it into the slot, and pressed PLAY…

First, there was a moment of confusion; some kind of color image quickly filled the screen—instead of the black & white I'd been expecting. What in blazes was this?

Then, confusion became consternation, as I realized that what I was seeing was a scene from some fairly recent contemporary drama. As a matter of fact, I quickly recognized *Jodi Foster's face* of all things. *She* certainly hadn't appeared in *Bride of Frankenstein*. Must have put in the wrong tape…

I popped it out again to check—and there was my own hand-written label: *Bride of Frankenstein.*

Hastily cramming it back into the machine, I firmly pushed a little, "Oh God, no!" into the back of my mind. Perhaps what I'd seen was seen was some leftovers on the end of the tape after *Bride.* Yeah, that's gotta be it. I'll just rewind all the way back to the beginning here and…

I pressed *rewind* and the machine spun backwards for not more than two seconds. This *was* the beginning.

Maybe I had inadvertently allowed a little junk at the beginning of the tape without realizing it, I guessed. Maybe I hadn't started recording at the exact beginning. I investigated this idea immediately…knowing full well, by now, that it wasn't true.

Seized with panic, I thought back to the day of the original recording and realized I hadn't broken out the little tab in the cassette…the ones that would have prevented accidental erasure. After that, it only took seconds to recognize that the only thing left on my *Bride of Frankenstein* tape now was a Jodi Foster movie called *Carny*. The whole unacceptable truth would have to be admitted. Tammy had been so fascinated with my technological wonder that she simply couldn't help herself. She'd been a little naughty and decided to try some home taping of her own, just to see if she could really do it, I suppose. *I* decided to collapse onto the carpet and pound my head against the floor for a while.

Tammy returned after ten minutes or so and found me sitting on the floor with a blank expression on my face. I think I managed to ask her what she'd done. From her response, I could tell she hadn't fully realized I'd been in earnest about that "leave the *record* button alone" business…and, after all, it's only a movie anyway. But now that she could see the dark circles beginning to form under my eyes and feel the bereaved atmosphere I was generating, she understood that perhaps she better just help me load up my stuff and go.

To be honest with you, I don't like to remember the rest of that weekend. I didn't go home to Atlanta. I didn't do much of anything. I recall driving back to the base in complete shock and then walking stiffly out the pier to the ship in dumb misery. I went straight to my bunk, got in it, and pulled the covers up over my head.

The Quest—December 1983

Now comes the real heart of my story—which took place about a year and a half later. I'd got out of the Navy and moved back to my home in Atlanta, staying with my parents for a while as I shifted back into civilian life. My original enlistment, however, called for another couple years in the Reserves—an obligation which includes a couple weeks active duty each year. In my particular case, this year's active duty was to involve a trip to New Orleans, Louisiana, where the Navy's personnel headquarters is located. I was to receive training on how to record attendance at reserve drill weekend (a dull subject which was destined, alas, to receive a dull treatment from my instructors). I would supply my own transportation to New Orleans (Dad loaned me a car) for which I would be paid 28 cents a mile and then be put up in Navy housing at the base. All this sounded fairly painless; I'd never been to Louisiana and, in a way, this would amount to two weeks paid vacation).

My alarm woke me up way before dawn on the morning of departure. I sleepily accomplished the Navy's "three S's" (military people will know what I mean) and was soon ready to get on the road. Before stepping out the door, however, I caught a glimpse of my big Sony Betamax sitting there on top of our 25" console—red digital numerals on the front (what won't they think of next?) spelling out 4:45 AM. And it suddenly occurred to me that perhaps I should just take that baby loose then and there and carry it to New Orleans with me. After all, strange TV stations in strange cities sometimes show strange stuff on TV; stuff you can't get at home. I considered the matter seriously; it might just be a good idea at that. But then the fuss and trouble came to mind. As I've already noted, VCR's were big in those days—heavy, too. Mine was like a full size Samsonite suitcase filled with Sackrete. It had lots of wires to unplug, too; even your remote had a wire on it in those days. And I'd likely make a great deal of noise getting it loose in the dark—probably wake up my parents. Yeah. Best forget it. Yet—hold on. What if I got way down there to New Orleans and something really wonderful *did* come on TV—and me without a recorder again? Then where would I be?

A little more sober thought settled things, however. I mean, what could they really show down there that it would just break my heart to miss? I thought of two or three flicks I'd certainly like to have, to be sure—but it wouldn't really *kill* me to miss them. As a matter of fact, I could think of only *one film*, in the whole nearly 90 year history of cinema, that actually would break my heart to miss—only one that would actually justify having lugged this delicate, cumbersome, expensive gizmo 500 miles southwest into the bayous. You know it—*The Bride of Frankenstein.*

The memory of my misadventure in King's Bay was still fresh enough to sting. The Bride of Frankenstein was more than just a movie, now. It had become a personal challenge. It had become a point of honor that one day, with God as my witness, I was going to get back onto that horse and ride it. And if I ever did, I'd sure as blazes remember to break out those damn little plastic tabs.

But what were the chances?—what hope that one of two or three independent TV stations in *the exact* distant city to which I was traveling would choose, during *the one* given fortnight in which I would happen to be there, might show this one, particular odd, old black & white monster movie? About a zillion to one, I concluded. In fact, the thought was ridiculous. Silly, in fact. So silly that it helped me make a sound, sensible adult decision, of the type my parents are still hoping I will learn to make someday. If *The Bride of Frankenstein* was the only film that would justify taking the VCR…well, the whole thing was settled. There was no point in taking it. I'd already proved, after all, that where that particular movie was concerned I had a phenomenal amount of luck, alright—all of it bad. I turned away, stepped out the door, locked it behind me, and drove to New Orleans.

My Dad's little blue Chevy Chevette preformed beautifully on the trip. I arrived at my destination by 5PM and had plenty of time for sightseeing, which I used to look the place over top to bottom. I was tucked into my Navy housing by midnight and never knew what hit me until it was time to get up for class the next morning.

Like I said earlier, the classes were dull—but hey, I had a car, right, and when the liberty bell rang I'd have the evening to explore the French Quarter, Basin Street, and so forth, right? Wrong. When school let out the first day I hopped into the driver's seat, turned the switch, and got nothing but a pitiful little click. I figured the battery was dead. Alas, two hours and two different sets of jumper cables later, I realized the whole unacceptable truth—my starter had gone kaput and I was stranded on the base.

Don't ask me why I went to New Orleans with only $10 in my pants. I was poor then. I'm pretty poor now. But in those days, I thought $10 was a lot of money. Of course, my meals and housing were on Uncle Sam. I wouldn't starve. And a DoD paycheck *was* coming eventually—one week from Friday, twelve days away, on the very day I was scheduled to go back home. In other words, I'd be able to leave the base just in time to buy a new starter, install it, and drive back home. Till then, I had no car, no money, and no friends (except the aforementioned Uncle Sam) to bum anything off of. I called my Dad and told him about the situation; he thought it was funny—which, I suppose, it was. But at the time, I fumed and cussed and then just basically resigned myself to spending the entire two weeks looking at TV in the Crew's Lounge (which, as it happened, looked very much like the one in which I had first seen that original *Bride of Frankenstein* TV spot back at King's Bay).

The next day I went to class again and the second session was, if anything, duller than the first. During a lunch break, I went down to the Navy Exchange to invest fifty cents of my remaining funds in a copy of TV Guide for the upcoming week. I causally opened the cover and started scanning the listings. The very first movie showing that week, on the very first day listed…was *The Bride of Frankenstein.*

I might write the cliché here and say that I couldn't believe my eyes. I might less a less hackneyed phrase and say that I doubted the evidence of my own senses. But the sad truth is that after the initial instant of stupefaction had passed I *did* believe my eyes. In fact, it only took a minute for that little notice—*Bride of Frankenstein,* Sat 12 Noon, Channel 13—to seem inevitable. In leaving that VCR in my parents room in Atlanta, I had flung the great and mighty city of New Orleans a challenge and she had risen to the occasion.

That night I took that preternatural little magazine back to my room and sulked. I don't mind saying that I almost cried. My fate in all this just seemed too cruel and unusual and just altogether too hard. I thought back to Jacksonville and Wayland Welden's silly-ass wife, and *Carny*. And now this on top of all that. I thought it was unfair, that's all, and I didn't care who knew it.

Yet slowly, as I lay there on my bunk clutching that *TV Guide* and gazing up at the ceiling, I realized that there was another way of looking at what had happened. Maybe that blown decision in my parent's bedroom wasn't my last chance. Maybe I was being given another decision to make. Maybe whatever occult forces had conspired together to put me through all this weren't actually bent on my humiliation. Maybe they were just raising the stakes. I know it sounds like a scene from a Donald Duck cartoon, but I thought I could hear two little voices giving me advice. One little voice seemed to be saying that I should knuckle under and give up. Or maybe *grow* up would be more accurate. It's only a movie anyway, for God's sake. You're 23 years old now and most people would think you're an idiot for even watching that creaky old movie, much less killing yourself trying to tape it. But the other little voice was quieter. You know, it's funny, but all my life all of the most miserably unhappy people I've ever known have always, nevertheless, been perfectly certain that this thing called "growing up"—which they most certainly *had* done—was the magical key to beatitude. Usually, the just wanted you to give up one of your dreams. Yeah, I pretty much had this growing up thing figured out by now. It was a bad deal. After all, I remember what I was like as a little kid—and I wasn't a bad guy at all! Sure, that little shaver needed to grow—to learn and expand and increase in favor with God and man—but he didn't need to be betrayed and destroyed and remade as a "grown up." My second little voice seemed to be saying, "Be true to that little guy. There's a reason all this is happening to you. You can lay down and die here…or get up and *fight!*"

Well, anyway, I made my decision. I know I made the right one, because if I'd chosen the other course this story would and *here*. And that would be awful. When you get done reading the rest, I bet you'll be glad it didn't.

The next day was Wednesday. That meant there were three and a half days until zero hour—*Sat 12 Noon, Chan 13*. In that time I'd have to dream up, plan, and be ready to execute some kind of way to tape a movie coming on TV in a strange city with no VCR, no blank videocassette, no TV of my own, and no money. Piece of cake.

My first inclination was to find some like-minded soul on the base—some other poor monster/fantasy/sci-fi movie nut—who might understand my situation, take me into his or her wing (if not home) and help me tape my movie when the appointed hour arrived. This proved, of course, way too much to hope for and nothing ever came of it. The closest

I ever got was to ask several of the guys on base if they knew anybody with a VCR. One finally said yes, but the subject turned out to be a big sports fan who bought the thing only in order to tape football games on the weekend. I knew better than to even ask.

By Thursday I was certainly getting a little antsy. I still had no idea what I was going to do—I merely reaffirmed, with a dreadful severity, that I would not simply lie in bed come Saturday morning and let a UHF signal carrying *The Bride of Frankenstein* pass *through my body* without forcing it to do so over my *dead* body. After class that day I asked around about VCRs in use on the base. There were a couple, as it happens, used for training during the week and happily idle on Saturdays. This sounded promising—at first. Maybe I could get permission…well, failing that, maybe I could sneak in or something…then find an antenna someplace…and then a blank videotape lying around (I had only $7 or so of my money left—blank tapes were at least 10 dollars back then!)…which I would have to steal when the taping was complete. It was, perhaps, fortuitous, considering all this, that I soon discovered the machines used on base were of the old U-matic type, totally incompatible with my system back home. So much for plan B.

Something would come to me before Saturday. I knew it would. None of this would make any sense at all if something didn't. And then…something did.

I sat up in bed that night as the plan jumped nearly complete into my mind. It was brazen. It was crazy. Surely it wouldn't...it couldn't really work?

But sure! Why not? With a little luck I didn't see why it shouldn't…by golly, it's GOT to work! That was it. That was the plan.

I needed a VCR to use. I couldn't rent, steal, or get permission to use someone else's. In other words, I needed one that was kind of…community property, so to speak. On that I could use without permission, and still not get thrown in jail. Where, in a big city like New Orleans, were there some VCR that anyone can touch, anyone can examine and even *use*…sort of? *In a department store!* Department stores are positively begging people to come and look at their VCRs. They spend thousands of dollars each month in advertising trying to get folks in to do so. It suddenly seemed to me that a properly motivated person could walk into a big department store, step up to a whole bank of VCRs, and then—while sort of trying one of them out real good—tape anything he wanted to. Certainly on lousy little 75 minute monster movie, anyhow. But waitasecond. What would I use for a videocassette? I still didn't have enough money to buy one. Got it! One or two of those demo machines in the stores always have a blank tape in them already, so the salespeople can make test recordings for potential customers (ahem) like myself. All I gotta do is find one that doesn't look too worn, pop it into one of the machines (might as well use the top-of-the-line model, don't you think?), set it to the proper channel, and then stall any snooping employees long enough to get that movie firmly onto ferrous oxide. Like I said before, piece of cake.

I set to work immediately; there was a lot to do before Saturday! The whole plan depended upon there being a department store within reasonable walking distance of the base. I went down to the quarterdeck and asked the Petty Officer of the Watch if knew of any malls or shopping centers nearby that might have a big Sears or J.C. Penney-type place in it. Happily, he informed me that one of the biggest malls in the state was about two-and-a-half miles from the main gate…a nice little stretch of the legs to be sure, but well within my limits. I took down the directions and after class the next day (Friday, with payday still exactly one week away), shot out the East Gate and took off at a brisk clip to preview *my VCR!*

The 45 minute walk wasn't at all unpleasant, to tell you the truth. The route was almost entirely along tree-lined suburban boulevards crowded with 1920s bungalow-style houses apparently owned by industrious Roman Catholic gardening enthusiasts (lots of flowers and saints). I remember that weekend as being a little on the chilly side, but the walk was warming and I took a sweater. It wasn't long before I'd reached the mall and picked out a likely-looking department store—part of a big regional chain. I didn't pause at all; I walked right in the door just like I had some legitimate business there.

The electronic department was not a disappointment. One whole wall was covered with TV sets and many of them were connected to a long shelf holding about 25 VCRs of various makes and models. I was politely greeted by a very lovely young saleslady who, to be honest, might not have been so convivial had she any inkling of the sort of lunacy I was really up to there in her tidy little corner of the store. I told I was "just looking" (perfectly true) and once she was gone, proceeded to scare up my not too warn videocassette. I then picked out a nice fancy Sony Beta machine with a $1,200 price tag, connected to a fine color TV which displayed New Orleans' own channel 13 just beautifully. Then, while the nice saleslady had her back turned, I hid the chosen videotape behind one of the TV sets to await my return the next morning…and went back to the base.

I went to bed about 8:30, setting the alarm for an early reveille the next morning, giving myself plenty of time before noon. I slept well that night, as I recall—a man with a mission.

D-Day arrived. I got up, had a brisk shower, a nice breakfast in the Mess Hall, and then took off for the mall real early—probably 7AM or so. Must have been, because I recall that I got there way, way too early. I hadn't wanted to take any chances, you know. As a result, I had to sit on the steps outside the entrance for an hour or two before the doors even opened. Then a killed at least another hour in a McCrory's, looking at dime store junk. I bought a Slurpee just because I didn't have anything else to do, then threw it away because—of course—it was way too early in the morning to drink a Slurpee.

I think the department store opened at 10:30. I went straight to the electronics department again. It was open all right, with the entire wall of TV screens playing the prelims to a football game which my Navy friend was no doubt happily recording in the privacy of his own home. None of the sales staff was on station yet. I thought about going on in, but then decided I didn't want to be seen just hanging around…yet. The Lord knows I'd be doing as much or more of that than I could hope to get away with later and so I quickly went to another part of the store and looked at furniture or something for another hour. Then, at 11:30, I decided I had better take up my post. I still needed to make sure that "my" videocassette was still available and I wanted to make a test recording or two with "my" machine, just to make certain all systems were go.

It took less than a minute for a conscientious salesperson to appear. This time, however, it was a big curly-headed man (I much preferred the pretty lady from the night before) who looked, I thought, uncomfortably like a grown-up "Butch" from the old *Little Rascals* films. He greeted me warmly enough, I suppose, and asked if he could be of any assistance. I said "Just looking" again (a little less truthfully this time) and he obligingly departed—for who knows how long. I switched the set connected to "my" VCR from the football contest over to Channel 13 which, according to *TV Guide*, should have been and was playing an old *Gilligan's Island* episode from 11:30 to Noon. I used it to test everything out fully.

Around 11:55, I was satisfied that I had done everything humanly possible to hold up my end of the deal, should the city of New Orleans actually choose to make good on her dare. I could see a big clock hanging over the sales desk across the way. Like Gary Cooper's Will Kane, I watched that big hand move along, slowly nearing *High Noon.* Being somewhat imaginative by nature, I could almost hear Tex Ritter singing.

Gilligan ended exactly on time. I solemnly pressed my borrowed Record button and sure enough, by golly, Channel 13 started showing *The Bride of Frankenstein.* And I, incredibly, was somehow there and somehow taping it.

Okay, it's all downhill from here. All I've gotta do is just keep that machine running and that big guy from asking any nosy questions. And try not to look conspicuous. For the next hour and a half (with commercials). All right, maye two hours. How hard could it be?

Alas, I was soon to find out.

I guess that big curly fellow asked if he could help me about ten times before the first commercial break happened. In fact, he was in the awfullest hurry to help me of anyone I ever met. Many times since then, in my various trials and tribulations, I have wished for someone half so eager to lend me their aid. Finally—and though I certainly don't justify what I did and can't recommend the practice generally—I determined that I would have to think up a lie, simply to prevent this man killing himself with helpfulness and ruining my whole enterprise.

Yes, I suppose it was somewhat less than entirely honest, but I finally told "Butch" that I was married. Yes, I was married and my wife was boring me to death in here looking at sofas. She was over in the furniture department and just couldn't make up her mind, what with that big selection and all, and, well sir, I finally just told her, "Honey, I'm going to go over and see if they have any TVs here and I'm going to watch the football game, that's all, while you try and make up your mind." You know how women are.

Butch smiled and seemed visibly to relax. Perhaps he could relate to my plight. And then I began to make good on my story by diverting a little of my attention from the one lonely TV set in all that sea showing a corny old black & white Frankenstein movie and directing it instead, to what appeared to be LSU versus Mississippi State or something. About which, if the truth were told, I cared less than nothing. I think Butch allowed (and I heartily seconded) that this certainly was an important game and that neither he nor I would want to miss a second of it, which was why he had all of these TVs in here showing that and not something else. In fact, Butch decided to stand there with me for a while and watch a bit of the game and talk some football with a man who obviously knew the game and appreciated it.

So we stood there talking football (I guess) the whole time Dr. Frankenstein planned his weird experiments with his old mentor Pretorius—well into the third reel, I believe. As a matter of fact, out of the corner of my eye I could see that the Monster was very nearly ready to sup with the old blind hermit before Butch again began to feel the call of duty and went back to the cash desk. But that Butch, I must say, really was a football fan. As he took my leave to assist another customer, he paused a moment to scratch and itch that had apparently been bothering him; he stopped at the one errant TV on the wall—the one with that goofy black & white stuff on it—and changed the channel to where it belonged.

My heart skipped a beat—but after the salesman was gone I realized he hadn't really done me any harm. The channel selector *on the VCR* is the only one that matters for taping (not the one on the TV) and that one, thank heaven, was still set on good old Channel 13. As a matter of fact, I decided to leave the TV on the football game for a while; the VCR would keep gobbling up my movie anyway and things would be less conspicuous without Karloff's pasty Frankenstein face poking out of all that pigskin. I'd wanted to follow along with the movie so that I could take the commercials out as I went, but I now realize that'd be pushing things a bit. Maybe I'd switch back later and take a few out near the end.

The middle of the movie was a breeze. My tall story seemed to keep most of the help quiet, and I was easily able to switch over to *Bride* from time to time to see how things were going. I began to get pretty confident, in fact. By the time the Monster kidnapped Elizabeth Frankenstein out of her boudoir, I figured I was pretty much home free. But I should have known I wasn't going to get off that easy…

I began to notice that an elderly lady had appeared down at the end of my row of VCRs…and was taking a keen interest in each and every one of them. She was fiddling with buttons in fact. It didn't take me long to realize that she was headed my way. She'd expect me to step away from "my" machine so that she could examine it. Was I willing to do that? She might insist and make a scene. I tried to puzzle out what to do as she got nearer and nearer. Boy, she's interested in these things! What does an old lady want with a VCR anyway? Is she going to tape cooking shows or something? Well, whatever she wants it for, the silly thing ought to know she doesn't need "my" fancy model with the audiophile sound. And there's no salesperson in sight to alert her of these facts, *of course.* They'd been all over me like white on rice the minute I walked into the door—where were the chuckleheads now? Now that they might actually do some good and point Grandma here at something she can use?

Just as the lady got to my position, a salesperson did, at last, materialize. It was another woman this time—middle-aged, spinstery, the kind of lady who might have been cast as the schoolmarm in an old Western. She introduced herself to Granny and pretty soon commenced telling her about all the wonders of home video recording, a subject about which it became clear the fascinated oldster had never gotten the first wind. The whole idea seemed a revelation to her. This inspired the saleslady to begin a spirited introduction to the subject which was warmly received by the senior; Granny never actually said, "Land sakes!" but that about sums up her end of the dialogue.

All this I patiently endured as I saw on my lone silvery island that Pretorius and his mad disciple were beginning their creation of the female monster—the grand climax and finale of *The Bride of Frankenstein.* I did not yet despair. After all, "my" machine was still whirring quietly, even if it was doing so within about four feet of two ladies who had probably whipped the tar out of better boys than me for watching trash exactly like the type that I was currently engaged in recording using expensive equipment other than my own. Yet when, after another minute or two, the schoolteacher actually stopped lecturing and chose "my" VCR to physically demonstrate the glories of this new era of home entertainment…when I actually saw her attempt to press *Play* only to discover that *Record* was already pressed…well, I nearly soiled my clothes. My heart stopped. With Granny patiently looking over my shoulder, the schoolteacher seemed puzzled for just an instant of time…and then she simply pressed the *Stop* button.

I shut my eyes in agony. So this was the end. Could I bear it?—to come so close, only to see the spirit of Jodi Foster triumph victoriously at last. I lifted my face—in a moment my eyes would be welling up with tears—and looked up to where, though my recorder had stopped, that haunted fleeting mirage of a movie would still be playing, taunting me. I looked up just in time…to see Channel 13 fading into a commercial break.

I had missed maybe eight or twelve seconds of the movie. Eight or twelve seconds of the movie good old Channel 13 would be showing the ending of, here in about *two and a half minutes.*

In about *150 seconds.*

Even now, all was not lost!

Granny and the schoolteacher had switched over to that damnable football game (with the dial that did, definitely, matter) and were now making a little demo tape on the end of my 85% finished *Bride of Frankenstein* cassette—just to prove to the lady, I suppose, that the miracle could in fact be performed.

This had to stop. That was all there was to it.

"Uh, ma'am?" I heard myself saying.

"Pardon?" Grandma turned away from her lecture.

"Yes, ma'am…I couldn't help noticing that you seem to be interested in buying a VCR."

"Well…maybe. Maybe one day."

"Well, if you don't mind my saying so, I own a VCR myself and I thought you might be interested in a personal recommendation."

"Really? Well, yes. I suppose so."

"Do you see *that* VCR?"

"Which…?"

"That one way down there on the end."

"Oh, yes. I see it. Yes."

"Well, that's the one I own. And it's great. A real workhorse. I've had it since 1978 and never had the first problem with it."

This was almost true. My machine *had* been perfect…but, well, there was a new model out now which had replaced it…and was supposed to be better, actually...but then I wasn't, to be honest, quite sure that the one I was pointing to was actually it.

90 seconds.

The schoolteacher reasserted herself.

"Do you mean the Panasonic?" she asked sharply.

"No, the Sony actually."

"Well, that *is* a good VCR," she admitted—but she still seemed determined to get a lot more of that football game on tape before she moved a muscle. I looked up and saw Channel 13 finish an *Armor-All* spot and go to one pushing *Hair Club for Men.*

60 seconds.

"Oh, yeah, I really think you couldn't do better than that Sony. Why don't you go down there and have a look at that one?"

"You really do?"

"I sure do. It's the best."

"Well...maybe I will," she observed, in a tone of voice which suggested next week rather than the right-damn-now I needed.

"Oh, yeah.." I continued, grasping for straws, my voice getting a little confused and plaintive as the seconds raced past. "That one's a winner, yes siree…I sure do…well, I know for a *fact* that the Sony…"

Hair Club turned into a promo for Channel 13's award-winning action packed *Eyewitness News at 6 and 11*. I sensed that it was now or never.

30 seconds.

"It's…it's…a lot cheaper, too! Do you know how much this one costs?"

Here, the schoolteacher shot me a dirty look.

"Um, no, I hadn't actually noticed."

"Twelve hundred bucks!"

Granny said nothing, but the look on her face told me I'd hit paydirt. Like a lot of folks back then, she probably looked on a VCR as a little accessory for your TV set—an extra along the lines of a remote control or a swiveling pine stand to put it on. Cost probably a hundred and fifty, two hundred bucks max. Right?

"Yeah, *one thousand two hundred dollars*, plus tax," I said, enunciating. "That other one, though…the one I told you about…that one's a real bargain."

Grandma's feet actually moved. She actually leaned in the direction I indicated.

15 seconds. I saw that *I* would have to actually move.

"Here, let me show you the one I mean." I stepped away from "my" machine, took Granny politely by the arm, and actually led the nice old lady down to the other end of the aisle. The saleslady followed, perhaps a little reluctantly, but she followed.

In a paroxysm of suppressed panic, I left them to their business and bolted (but *casually*) back down to my end, just as the announcer's voice said, "And now for the exciting conclusion of *The Bride of Frankenstein…*"

There was no time to rewind over the schoolteacher's test tape of LSU vs. Mississippi State; that little fragment is there to this day. All I could do was to turn the dial back to Channel 13 and let the machine keep right on taping. Which the lovely, hideously-expense thing did very admirably.

Without further incident, the movie's big finish played out beautifully onto "my" tape. It was more wonderful than I remembered. Elsa hissed at Boris, Colin Clive escaped with Valerie Hobson, but Ernest Thesiger belonged dead, and so the whole house came down with a crash and great was the fall of it. Then, the sight I had ached for for nearly two hours (if not two years) finally filled the screen: Universal's buzzing little airplane circling a misty globe, hanging in a Vitaphone void. I pressed Stop, then Eject…and once again I held a videocassette of The Bride of Frankenstein in my hands.

And yes, I took out my car keys immediately and violently removed those silly *tabs!*

I couldn't take any chances by celebrating right there in the store. I wasn't out of the woods yet—not by a long shot. That borrowed videocassette didn't belong to me. It had my movie on it now, but it wasn't my property and I had no money with which to try and buy it. Wouldn't have for another week. I was suddenly seized by the insane temptation to try and get out the door with it using the old "five fingered discount"—but I put that urge down immediately. If anything was likely to cause this whole dream to sour into a big ugly nightmare it was something like that—messing around with the rules of the game like that. No sir, the challenge had been not to grow up, to launch into this wild Don Quixote crusade on a wing and a prayer—and you can't pray while you're stealing. I realized I was going to have to do this one by the book. Which meant that that videocassette was going to have to stay right there in that department store until I had the money to pay for it fair and square.

So I found another secure spot (I hoped!) behind one of the TV sets and, when nobody was looking, I stuck my tape of *The Bride of Frankenstein* into it, turned around bravely and walked out of the store just as empty-handed as I'd been when I got there.

The next week was video purgatory. I had to sit through those incredibly dull Navy personnel classes all day every day while my tape sat there in that store, naked and vulnerable. The more I thought about it the more panicked I became. I'd left it out in plain sight; I'd left it where the magnetism from the back of the TV would erase the tape; I'd left it where the heat from all that equipment would melt it. I'd had it *in my hands*…and I'd left it. By the time payday finally did come around, I was half convinced that there was nothing left to go back for.

But payday did finally come. The interminable classes ended and I was able to cash my check, fix my car, and patiently finish up my affairs at the base. Now I was free. The open road to Atlanta beckoned. But I had one very important stop to make along the way. I drove slowly and deliberately make to the mall—a free man with money in his pocket.

Butch was behind the counter when I made my triumphant return to the electronics department. He seemed to recognize me, but since I had made it abundantly clear last week that I wasn't an imminent threat to spend any money and was—if experience was any guide—likely to be there a while, he did not hurry over to greet me. I was able to walk over to my hiding place unmolested and to reach behind the TV set to find…nothing!

I almost died…before realizing that perhaps it had been the TV on the row beneath this one.

I checked and there I found, neither melted nor destroyed nor irradiated, my *Bride of Frankenstein* tape.

Butch had a somewhat stern look on his face as I approached the check-out.

"Uh…hi!"

"What can I do for you?"

"Well, uh…this is kind of hard to explain but…I'd like to buy this videotape." I held up my naked cassette… no wrappings or price tag…not even a cardboard jacket.

"Where'd you get that?" he asked, rather shortly.

"Well, you see…"

Come on, kid. You're Don Quixote. Tell him the truth.

"Uh, you may remember that I was in here last Saturday…" And how.

There was no hint of a smile or any such thing on Butch's face.

"And, well, this is a demo tape from your store here…and it has something recorded on it that I'd like to have. I want to buy it from you."

"Not for sale."

I paused, trying not to look horror-stricken.

"Why not?"

"Against store policy."

"What is?"

"Selling a demo tape like that."

What kind of a policy was that!?

"Why?"

"If you want a blank videotape you'll have to pay full price like everybody else."

Full price? So that *was* the problem. He thought I was trying to get a videotape on the cheap!

"I'm willing to pay full price for this one!"

"You are?"

I was. As soon as Butch understood that I wasn't trying to get some sort of price break on something he became a different man. If he thought I was weird for wanting to pay full price for a well-used demo, he kept it to himself. I happily paid him the $9.95 for a brand new L-500 fresh out of stock which he carefully unwrapped and put into one of the VCRs as a new demo. And then he gave me leave to depart with my treasure.

I can still remember the flush of sheer joy that swept over me as I walked out of the department store carrying that tape, through the mall and out to my fully repaired and gassed-up Chevy Chevette. I kid you not—the minute I cranked up the car and turned out of the parking lot onto the road home, a shaft of sunlight burst through what had been, for most of my two weeks in New Orleans, a gray overcast sky and it bathed me, my car, and my videotape and left it where I could look at it—on the passenger seat next to me—all the way home.

And I drove the eight hours back to Atlanta, bringing home from Louisiana the very last thing on earth I would have believed it possible to have gained there.

Epilogue - Summer 1987

About four years after my supposed happy ending in New Orleans came this horrifying epilogue.

It was 1987. I was sharing a rented house with two good friends. We'd been able to put together, on a low budget, a pretty impressive little movie room there by combining our resources: several VCRs, a nice TV, some not-bad stereo equipment, and a library of about 300 movies…one of which was my little prize wrested from the Creoles and Cajuns. We lived there quite happily for several months before I made the momentous decision which, Rod Serling might have put it, was to be that last move in a chess game I had been playing since the day I first saw that commercial at King's Bay; a chess game being played out…in the Twilight Zone.

One lazy afternoon that summer, I decided to while away some time by watching one of my favorite movies, and by basking in some very happy memories. In other words, I decided to pull out my hard-won tape of *The Bride of Frankenstein* and have a nice long look at it—two and a half minutes of football game and all.

I didn't like to clutter up my video tapes with a lot of ugly labels; I put small numbers on them instead and recorded which number corresponded to what movie in a nice neat book. So on that fateful day, I looked up Bride of Frankenstein in the book and found it listed as #53. After a moment I had #53 in hand; I casually popped it into the machine, ready to sit back and gloat.

There was a moment of confusion as a color image came up rather than the black & white I'd been expecting. Perhaps I'd put in the wrong tape.

There was a moment of consternation as my eyes registered what I was seeing as a scene from some fairly contemporary drama. Perhaps this was something on the tape after *The Bride of Frankenstein.*

Finally, there was the moment when I recognized the face of none other than Ms. Jodi Foster. And I knew, with a terrible certainty, that I was watching *Carny.*

I silently sat down on the couch and stared. Yes, there was Jodi Foster in Carny—on the tape that was supposed to be my prize from New

Orleans. I goggled. I gaped. I had nothing to say.

I became numb. I kept looking at the screen but Jodi Foster never went away. There she remained, on the very tape I had kissed as I sped away from the department store. There was Jodi Foster in *Carny*—on the tape I had labored like Hercules to get, the tape with which I had defied the gods of probability, snatching out of the very jaws of impossibility my Holy Grail, my Northwest Passage, my Golden Fleece. Wait—perhaps that was it. Perhaps, like Icarus, my victory had been impious. Perhaps my owning a tape of *The Bride of Frankenstein* just cosmically wasn't meant to be. Perhaps I had sinned in contriving my schemes so arrogantly and so cleverly and was now being sent this hateful miracle as a punishment. Perhaps this awful, impossible, inescapable Jodi Foster movie would now hound me forever through time and eternity, like some cinematic Flying Dutchman, ready to vex and confound me whenever and wherever I might dare to suppose that a tape of *The Bride of Frankenstein* could be mine.

Far-fetched? So is this whole ridiculous yarn—and yet everything in it is true, so help me. Surely the odds were nothing less than astronomical against *Bride of Frankenstein* being shown the very week in New Orleans I'd been so sure it wouldn't. And yet the impossible had happened—and I was no longer prepared to call anything under the sun impossible. Who will blame me if I entertained notions of curses, plagues, divine vendettas? Could you, my friend? What other explanation was more inherently plausible?

That I was losing my mind?

This terrible idea was just beginning to seriously commend itself…when I heard the guffaws from the kitchen.

My roommates had had enough. They stumbled into the movie room wracked with tears, roaring with delight. And I knew that I had been had.

Seems my roommate and dear friend Bryan had noticed, some months before and during a routine perusal of the weekly *TV Guide*, that some irresponsible local station in Atlanta had scheduled a showing of *Carny*. And Bryan had already heard the first two sections of this fable you've been reading. Within his twisted mind was hatched the following diabolical plot. He would tape the hated *Carny* on a fresh new videotape and then steal my precious *Bride* from off its shelf, hide it in his own room, switch a few little numbers around, and then bide his time—waiting for the inevitable day when I must get the itch to take down my prize and attempt to watch it. It was a beautiful, perfect, perfectly dastardly plan. He had only to hope that he was actually home when the moment of truth at last arrived. When that moment did finally arrive, I guess the awful silence through which he must have heard Jodi Foster's voice suddenly cut, let him know that his labor had not been in vain.

Bryan recently told me that he always felt this joke was something of a bust; it didn't get the big vocal reaction from me that he expected. I assured him that it had worked to perfection, better than he could possibly have hoped. My silence was that of a man questioning his own sanity, of a man looking down into a pit opening under his feet. And hey, any practical joke that can get your best friend to do that has gotta be a Grade-A bang-up success. Am I right?

Any lessons to be learned from my quest for *The Bride?* I don't know. When I look back on the story I get a feeling similar to one I often get when reading history. Sometimes when you read about certain great events in world history you get the oddest feeling that you're watching a show being put on for your benefit or even a lesson being taught. History is full of impossible coincidences and situations too full of meaning to have actually occurred. Author Bruce Catton, America's greatest Civil War historian, wrote that certain chapters of our past made him feel "as if a legend had been created to express some obscure truth that could not otherwise be stated." Perhaps this is what Shakespeare meant when he wrote, "All the world's a stage, And all the men and women merely players…"

I guess, in my own small way, I feel like my whole little quest was like that, sort of pre-planned from the beginning to teach me a lesson. What was the lesson? I don't think there's any way to separate it from the story itself. You either get it from the story or you don't get it.

Or then again, maybe Somebody just wanted to give me a really great yarn to tell at parties.

Anyhow…anybody up for *The Bride of Frankenstein?* I'll make the popcorn!

Originally published in *Wonder #8,* Spring 1992

WHY 2001 WON'T BE LIKE "2001"

2001 is pretty much here.

In fact, when astronaut John Glenn makes his much-heralded return to space this October, Hollowood's magic date with futurity will be a mere 27 months away. What will the 77 year old Glenn see when he finally gets back to Earth orbit? His last visit, after all, was 36 years ago. Like any wayfarer, one expects that Glenn will be curious to find out how the old neighborhood's been getting on in his absence. What's changed up there in half-a-lifetime?

According to the movie—Stanley Kubrick's monumental *2001: A Space Odyssey*—Glenn should find a massive orbital space station 220 miles above sea level. He ought to be able to dock there, doff his helmet, and check his bags at the Hilton Hotel before strolling down to Howard Johnson's Earthlight Room for a quick bite. There ought to be picture phones and stewardesses and a nice hot zero-gravity shower. And there ought to be connecting flights to the Moon—to *Clavius Moonbase*, a permanent colony where heroic men of science are alreay making plans for a manned voyage to Jupiter.

There ought to be...but, of course, there won't. To astronaut John Glenn, "2001" will look just like 1962. As a matter of fact, Glenn's upcoming shuttle mission is, for all practical purposes, identical to his Project Mercury exploit of long ago: *go up into space, make a few orbits around the world, take some pictures, and then come back down.* To be fair, there is a space station of sorts—the ramshackle Russian MIR, crippled, financially-busted, and barely inhabitable; nobody's idea of a space-going Hilton. Despite having a few footprints on it, the Moon is also pretty much as it was during the Kennedy era. According to a recent report, if the order for a return trip to the Moon were given today, it would take nearly as much time to accomplish as it did the first time aound...and vastly more money. In short, it has become clear that the bold predictions of Kubrick's masterpiece (30 years old this year, by the way) were entirely illusory. It may have been the last word in realism in its day, but we now know that *2001*'s vision of the future turned out to be about as accurate as *Flash Gordon.*

And why is that?

Yesterday's Tomorrow

Oddly enough, most space movies of the 1950s seemed to make just the opposite error. The classic *Forbidden Planet*, for example, opens with these words: "In the final decade of the 21st century, men and women in rocket ships landed on the moon…" Now, *Forbidden Planet* is an extremely intelligent space film—the *2001* of its day, in fact, with MIT scientists vetting the script every step of the way. Yet in predicting an event which was destined in real life to happen just 13 summers later, *Forbidden Planet* missed its mark by at least 121 years. Similarly, Walt Disney's famous *Man in Space* TV programs display to modern viewers the same colossal conservatism. Here (circa 1957) a mere orbital pass *around* the Moon is presented as a distant dream to be witnessed by our fortunate grandchildren. And yet, incredibly, the technical advisor for these films was Dr. Wernher von Braun—the man chosen to head the design team for the Apollo launch vehicle slightly less than *four years later*. So didn't these earlier prophecies, in their own way, fail just as badly as those of *2001*?

Perhaps. But these days more and more space historians are siding with Walt Disney and *Forbidden Planet.*

It's true, of course, that man did go to the Moon is the year of our Lord 1968. With 2001 still splashed across the Cinerama screens of the home world, men from the planet Earth traveled a quarter-million miles through space aboard Apollo 8 to rendezvous with another celestial body for the first time in history. This achievement can never be minimized. But in the 25 years which have elapsed since the final Apollo mission, it has become increasingly clear that America's interplanetary adventures of the 1960s and 70s (grand as they undoubtedly were) constitute something of an historical anomaly. Though at the time these were seen as the dawning moments of a new age—the confidently announced "Space Age"—we're now beginning to understand that they actually fit far more comfortably into the closing chapters of another historical epoch: the Cold War.

"Apollo was this incredible Cold War gambit for international prestige," says Andrew Chaikin, author of the definitive space history *A Man on the Moon.* "First and foremost, the reason Kennedy said we should go to the Moon was because he really wanted to make an impression on the world that the U.S. system was the best system." Likewise, filmmaker and space expert Tom Hanks (star of *Apollo 13* and producer of the recent HBO miniseries *From the Earth to the Moon*) also puts a finger on the driving force behind America's Moon trip: "There was a national will and a mobilization of forces that could only come about by an executive order. We can sit around now and say we're going to Mars someday, but it could be 120 years from now. Kennedy made it necessary to hire hundreds of thousands of people and develop all this technology. Without that, we probably wouldn't have been to the moon until the mid-1970s—maybe not even until the 1980s." Hanks' partner, producer Ron Howard, is even more dour: "In a lot of ways, the Cold War effort that propelled the space program at that time probably pushed us as human beings along much faster than we would have gone. I mean, there are people within NASA, and the Soviet space community as well, that really feel that if we had just gone along at our normal course, we probably would've gone to the Moon in maybe 2100, not 1969."

To put it shortly, the space thinkers of the 1950s had been right: in the natural order of things a voyage to the Moon belongs to "the final decade of the 21st century." It was only the ideological passions ignited by a "Space Race" which somehow yanked such a voyage out of Walt Disney's Tomorrowland backward into the post-World War II world created at Yalta.

Legends of the Fall

This disconcerting admission—that humanity's greatest adventure was, in one very important sense, nothing but a publicity stunt—is sobering, but not, to students of history, very shocking. Truth be told, a good many of our finest hours have been entangled with questions of national bravado and filthy lucre. Even Christopher Columbus went to America not "because it is there," but because it happened to get in the way of a projected trade route to India. Yet there's one crucial difference: Columbus' voyage truly did mark the opening of an epoch—the Great Age of Exploration. In the first 25 years after his 1492 landing (and through the efforts of giants like Balboa, Magellan and Cabot) Columbus saw his world double in size; new life forms (if you will) and new civilizations had been contacted, and a whole New World had begun to be colonized. In contrast, the first quarter-century after Apollo just hasn't amounted to much. Once again, Tom Hanks puts it well: "When I was a kid I just assumed that by 1998 we'd be traveling in Pan Am space clippers. Pan Am was actually taking reservations, and I called up and got one. Now, never mind that there are no space clippers, there's not even a Pan Am anymore! Anybody in July of 1969 would have said, 'We're going to have colonies on the Moon, and we'll figure out a way to get there cheaper, and we'll have dome cities.' They all just assumed that as soon as you discover the way to get there you keep going back, just like we did with Alaska, California, and the Ohio valley. In retrospect, it's more surprising that we stopped going to the Moon than that we got there in 1969."

And this, of course, is precisely the point at which *2001* was taken off guard. Arthur C. Clarke (the noted scientist who wrote the screenplay) based *2001*'s predictions solidly upon the sober projection of current trends...which, alas, were at the time thoroughly fluky and altogether artificial. At the time the movie was written both America and Russia were flinging dollars and rubles into the void at a truly astonishing rate—a rate which anyone should have been able to see was totally unsustainable for any length of time. Likewise, Clarke seems to have been unable to grasp the fact that all of this spending (despite a good deal of diplomatic PR to the contrary) was *military* spending. Just as the war was *cold*, the only shots being fired in it were *moon shots*. But being fired they were, and less at the Moon that at each other. Congress did not approve these billions in an idealistic effort to make a "giant leap for mankind." They did it to *defeat the bad guys*...and once the bad guys were defeated Project Apollo had served its purpose. This is not to say that there weren't scientific goals—and magnificent ones—but simply to insist that the objective which actually paid the bills was the conquest of communism, not the conquest of space.

This hard unromantic truth proved to be *2001*'s undoing as prophecy. The very fact that the lunar landing *had* been accomplished so early—well within the lifetimes of many who remembered Kitty Hawk—this fact alone produced a startling (and as it turns out *inflated*) sense of human progress. After all, with a man actually standing on the Moon to assure us that it was so, who could doubt that some kind of "giant leap" had in fact been made? But the domed cities, the Moon colonies, the Howard-Johnson's-in-space never came. They never came because, in actuality, we jumped the gun on our Space Age. Historically speaking, it was a false start, which ended on July 24, 1969, when NASA achieved its first, greatest, and only true objective: *"to land a man on the Moon and return him safely to the Earth."*

All Dressed Up and No Place to Go

Yet what about today's on-going space program? Isn't there a highly advanced re-usable space shuttle in service? Don't we still rocket men and women boldly into the heavens as the real 2001 draws near?

There is and we do. What we lack is any particularly urgent *reason* for doing it.

With the Great Russian Bear mortally wounded, NASA kept the doors open during the late 1970s by re-inventing itself. This being the age of détente, the quixotic, long-haired rationale of *Scientific Discovery* was moved to the fore, replacing the now slightly embarrassing notion of defeating the bad guys. Not surprisingly, the budget was drastically cut. Then, as we entered the hustling Reagan era, the new Space Shuttle system was put into operation. In reality, the Space Shuttle was a conceptual relic from the von Braun *Man in Space* days; a mere link in a chain which was originally supposed to end at the planet Mars. The Shuttle, in other words, was actually going to *shuttle* something—parts and labor to a great Space Wheel where a whole majestic fleet of Mars ships would be constructed. But Mars (a natural enough target for the Scientific Discovery crowd) simply made no sense at all from a practical standpoint—especially since there was soon no one to beat in a race to it. And so the Shuttle was re-imagined for the 80s as a floating product-development laboratory. As long as we keep sending this hideously expensive thing up, we were solemnly assured, wonderful technological blessings would trickle down from high-Earth orbit.

What was missing in all this was a certain sense of truthfulness. By the late 1990s, as the number of Shuttle missions steadily neared 100, even the most curious of us began to wonder just how many science experiments you can actually do up there in that high, tight circle. Even NASA administrator Daniel Goldin recently admitted that the Space Shuttle is "a marvelous transport system…without a destination." And did John Glenn and company really strap themselves to those gigantic flying bombs merely in order to enrich the magnates of Silicon Valley? Do any of these earnest justifications represent our real reasons for being in space—much less a realistic ground for continuing to support such efforts?

Today, the mounting pressure to give solid answers to these questions is bringing another '50s space fantasy a bit closer to reality: the permanent orbiting space platform. Though nothing at all like *2001*'s incredible city in the sky, when *Space Station Freedom* was first proposed fifteen years ago, it did represent a serious attempt to do something serious in space. Three draconian budget cuts later however, Space Station Freedom has somehow morphed into the *International Space Station*; about half the size originally planned and largely symbolic in nature. Arthur C. Clarke himself recently felt the need to comment on the progress of his intellectual step-child: "I have ambivalent feelings about the International Space Station. I may be biased, of course, because in *2001* it was a nice rotating ring with artificial gravity—whereas the space station plan now is, frankly, an orbiting pile of junk from the look of it." Space savant Freeman Dyson, of the *Institute for Advanced Studies*, puts the current state of things more bluntly still: "The [Space Station] project is being driven by politicians for political reasons. It's such a large undertaking and such an important source of jobs—it's just a huge welfare program for the aerospace industry. Whether it's actually any use or not has never really been the question." And future voyages to Mars? Dyson continues: "I don't think we're going to Mars in the next 50 years. I just don't see any point in having a huge expenditure of public money on just a prestige trip to take a couple of people to Mars and bring them back—which is all you could do with the present technology. I don't think it makes any sense."

Dyson is, of course, correct here—"prestige trips" don't make any sense. And yet the entire Apollo Moon program was planned, financed, and actually carried out in order to accomplish just such a prestige trip. Why did it work then and why won't it work now? The answer is simple: *the presence or absence of a genuine, honest-to-goodness, get-off-your-duff motivation.*

Lost in Space

Failing the discovery of some such motivation, space exploration in the 21st century seems destined, like MacArthur's old soldier, not to be killed but simply to fade away.

Will such a motivation be found? In one sense, the question itself proves that we've been putting the cart before the horse; if one actually has a need then one won't be scrambling about looking for it. But is it possible that we have needs which are being obscured—actual motivations for space exploration that are currently being addressed in contrary ways?

One important historical example strongly suggests that this may be the case. Looking back into the records of this kind of inquiry, one notices immediately that the early space philosophers of our century spent very little time rhapsodizing about naked scientific discovery…and none whatever about any commercial prospects. No, what seems to have chiefly inspired geniuses like Haldane, Stapledon, Wells, and Bradbury (certainly no enemies of science) was one of the same considerations which animated the early terrestrial explorers: the hope of colonization. With the specter of overpopulation beginning to loom ahead, the possibility of colonizing other planets such as Mars forcefully presented itself to these early visionaries. If man's home world is not enough, they theorized, then our ingenuity will carry us across the void to new spheres just as it carried our ancestors across the fearful seas to what seemed a countless earthly frontier. But starting about 1970, this original motive begins to vanish from the discussion. Even as overpopulation begins to be described by the media in downright apocalyptic terms ("The Population Bomb," etc.), even as the fiery rockets of science fiction become an everyday reality, space colonization is cleared from the table. The population problem begins to be addressed in other ways—cheaper, quicker, more ruthless ways. And thus one of the most important traditional incentives for exploration short-circuits in a futuristic re-enactment of Frederick Jackson Turner's famous *Closing of the Frontier*. Is it merely a coincidence that 1970 is roughly the year when NASA began to lose its way?

In any event—and with or without sufficient motivation—astronaut

John Glenn is scheduled to return to outer space next month. Surely all true Americans—indeed, anyone with an ounce of poetry in their souls—must rejoice and wish him, once again, *Godspeed.* Just as he was in 1962, this Ohio farm boy who will race across our night skies is a perfect mirror of everything good about our nation. It's no reflection on these modern Lewis & Clarks that most of us on the world leave behind stand paralyzed in indecision, unable or unwilling to go where they lead.

But unfortunately, it really must be said…for our children' sake and as a wake-up call…

2001 is here—and America's most eagerly watched space venture is a re-run.

Originally published by *Gadfly Magazine,* Summer 1998

STRANGER THAN YOU THINK

Let me take a moment to paint you a word picture.

The year is 1914. The place is Santa Rosa, California: that golden, All-American small town sixty or so miles north of San Francisco. There, under a cobalt blue sky, dry fragrant breezes drift off the surrounding vineyards to bathe rows of Victorian houses with a breath of air like that which must have come off the treetops of Eden. Near the center of the town, on a neat, green little ball field behind the Methodist Church, a shy, buck-toothed young man named Leroy Ripley stands on the pitcher's hill serving up the best split-finger fastball in the Golden State League.

It's the fifth and final game of the regional championship. Whoever wins this one will take the train to Frisco to face the boys from San Jose. The home town crowd cheers Ripley on, a native son making quite a name for himself lately in bush-league ball. Leroy isn't used to the spotlight. He's quiet by nature, unsure of himself; afraid of girls. During the off-season he polishes tombstones down at the local monument works. But Ripley loves baseball like Frankie loved Johnny. And he has an embarrassing secret—deep inside he cherishes the notion of one day pitching the deciding game of the World Series. He knows it's one chance in a million. Yet there, sitting in the dugout watching the game, he can see Dunnigan, the big league scout…

The sun is shining warm on his shoulders now. The scenario is just the sort of thing they dream up for the dime sports novels: bottom of the ninth, two outs, runners at second and third, a 3-2 count, and Santa Rosa clinging to a one-run lead. Finley, monster outfielder for the rival Fresno team (and currently batting every bit of .346) stands sixty feet away with a smile on his lips which is vaguely insulting.

The pitcher shrugs off two signs from his catcher. Then Leroy Ripley takes a slow, deep breath...winds...and delivers.

Now, fast-forward twenty-five years.

The year is 1939. The place: Mamaroneck, New York. On a snowy, rocky island in Long Island Sound a tall granite house juts up against a black wintry sky. Its windows are ablaze with light but they rattle and moan against the frigid north wind coming in over the water. Inside, twenty elegant evening guests have just finished the largest and most authentic Chinese dinner this side of Peking and are now beginning to hit heavily their host's impressively stocked bar. And who can blame them? The BION Mansion is a haunted castle and they are locked in for the night.

These are the rich and famous of their day—movie stars, radio personalities, writers, intellectuals, Hall of Fame ballplayers. But even the most jaded of them must feel uneasy about the prospect of spending the night under this roof; for BION is a veritable Pandora's Box waiting to spring open. All around them, in every niche, on every square foot of wall space, their imperious host proudly displays his "collection"—the booty of a world-wide search for the weird, the disturbing, the occult, the impossible. Half a million miles and more has this mad magician traveled to gather up his private museum, which currently includes an assortment of authentic shrunken heads, Lucretia Borgia's poison cabinet, a magnificent display of primitive magic artifacts (including a pin-studded voodoo doll from Haiti), and the world's largest private collection of slightly used torture devices from the Middle Ages.

The lights will go out soon. The guests will retire to several lavishly appointed bedrooms, just down the hall from where the original Iron Maiden of Nuremberg stands quietly with her door just ajar. Will the guests lie still and listen for the ghosts? Will they creep surreptitiously downstairs in order to see what happens at BION after midnight? Will they pull the covers up over their heads?

Whatever they decide to do, the Master of BION is sitting up tonight with a 400 year-old leather bound copy of Lao Tse. Propped comfortably in his own bedroom under a hanging bird-shaped fertility fetish gained on an excursion to New Guinea, he carefully adjusts his small silver reading glasses. It's no secret that he keeps a harem of six lovely Chinese wives here with him at BION; but tonight the Master will sleep alone, enjoying the warm awareness that his guests are snuggled quietly under the shelter of his hospitality, while winter blasts the night without.

Finally, Leroy Ripley closes his book and turns out the light. He sleeps almost immediately. Perhaps he will dream tonight; about the sun, about Santa Rosa, about pitching the deciding game of a great World Series...

When I was ten years old something happened to me that changed my life. I don't know—is it a common thing to be able to put your finger on a single day that, perhaps more than any other, seemed to permanently shape your outlook on life? I believe I can do just that. I don't remember the actual calendar date or anything like that...but just about everything else about that long ago summer's day is hallucinogenically vivid in my memory.

I had a neighborhood friend named Max whom I nearly worshipped. He was two years older than me and quite simply the smartest, savviest, hippest thing alive. He was found reading books by Jules Verne—whereupon *I* read every book by Jules Verne I could get my hands on. He read other science-fiction books, too; by people with names like Heinlein, Silverberg, Asimov, and Blish. Books that seemed so adult...well, so adult that I wondered if you might not have to be twelve to understand them. But by far the coolest thing Max was into was *science.* Max had a basement, you see—cool and dark, like an alchemist's cave. In this basement his Dad (also very hip) had helped Max to set up a *bone fide* laboratory, making him, I think, the only kid I'd ever heard of who had a laboratory. There, spread out across some wide wooden workbenches, was the biggest chemistry set I'd ever seen—surely the entire product line of the Edmund Scientific Company, blessings on their memory. And get this...Max actually seemed to know what to do with it! And he had a microscope, too! And he shot off Estes model rockets! And he had his own subscription to *Scientific American*! Egads. It was all mightily impressive to me.

Under Max's influence I asked for and received my own chemistry set for Christmas. Made some really dreadful messes as I (and my mother) recall. But Max—he didn't just fool around with science. Max was a true believer. He was a science booster, a science salesman, a veritable science *evangelist.* Max said that everything that had ever been worth the trouble of doing had been done by a scientist. Science was a crusade. Science was the heroic agent that had reached down into the slime and lifted a bunch of monkeys up to knowledge and dignity. Science would someday usher in the new and glorious age of human godhood.

Now those of you with an analytical bent will perhaps have noticed that this scientific faith of Max's is not entirely compatible with traditional Christian belief. I had not. At this point in my life I was still being dutifully taken to the Baptist Sunday School each and every week and had never seen any particular reason to doubt the things I was being taught there. That I had never actually *seen* God, or Jesus, or any angels or devils, bothered me not one whit. After all, practically all of what a ten year-old believes is accepted solely because some older person has said that it is so. When, therefore, Max began preaching the glories of the scientific outlook I readily added this new gospel to my existing stock; not noticing or particularly caring about the contradictions. Not, that is, until this one particular summer morning.

On this special morning, as I recall, Max and I were looking at some pickled fleas (or something) under the mighty eye of his 500X lens when—

oh, so casually—my 12 year-old role model dropped his bombshell:

"Hey, I read in one of my magazines yesterday that an astronomer has found *Heaven* with his telescope."

"Say what?"

"Yeah, some astronomer has found a bright star that he says is the center of the galaxy. He thinks we're all going to go there when we die. He says that if he had a larger lens he might could see God himself..."

I didn't know what to say. Probably my mouth hung open for a minute or two. Recall that I was only ten, too young to realize that this "astronomer's" discovery was being printed for laughs, in the spirit of the *National Inquirer*; my inquiring little mind took the proposal with complete Socratic seriousness. In fact, I began to wrestle with the implications. Did this mean that astronauts might one day be able to *fly* to this place and have a nice long chat with, say...Abe Lincoln? With my great-grandpa? With Jesus Himself? Could we maybe get into radio contact with this place now and ask God all our questions? Perhaps Max would now start going to church with me on Sundays. Truly, the mind boggled.

Yet before it could get too very boggled my friend dropped his second casual earth-shaker of the day; which, I guess, messed me up even worse than the first:

"It's all baloney, of course. Everybody knows there's no such thing as God."

Now, it wasn't, I don't think, that I had never heard of atheism before. No, I definitely remember having heard rumors about a few away benighted souls who deny the existence of their own Creator. But this was different. This was *someone I knew*....one of my personal friends. And worse, it was my role model! It's probably a bad metaphor to use in this context, but here I was, committed to the belief that Max walked on water...and him an atheist!

He let the remark hang artfully in the air. I was too stunned to attempt a reply. By the time I'd recovered enough to begin framing some sort of tentative protest—to mildly assert that I did, after all, know at least a few people that Max's "everybody" didn't seem to cover—he was ready to turn his casual remark into a full-fledged attack on all of my backward little superstitions.

"Yeah, science has disproved all that God stuff years ago. Nobody with any education believes in it anymore. That went out with Sea Serpents and Santa Claus."

Now he was getting personal. My Mom & Dad believed in God, for crying out loud!

"Max, don't you think..."

"Waitasecond. You're not saying you still buy all those fairy tales are you?"

"...well, I don't know if..."

"Listen, if you're going to be a scientist you've got to get with the program. Don't you know that that's what all this is about? I mean, it's the great titanic struggle against the forces of repression, for Chrissake!"

"It is?"

"Of course. Look, have you ever seen God? I mean actually seen him?"

"No."

"Ever heard his voice? I mean, an actual, audible voice out of the sky?"

"I guess not."

"Well, there you go. Those were just things somebody told you to scare you into doing what they wanted you to. A scientist doesn't believe in something until it's proved to him...right under his nose. Listen, back in the old days people were superstitious. They believed in evil spirits and four-leaf clovers and angels and all that kind of stuff. You know why? Because they hadn't learned about science. They were still afraid of the unknown. They didn't know the great secret we know..."

"What secret is that?"

"That there's *a scientific explanation for everything*."

There's a scientific explanation for everything. There-is-a-scientific-explanation-for-everything. Astounding. I'd never heard anything like it Max had a *creed*; he knew what it was and he stated it—right up front, so that everyone could try it out for themselves. There is a scientific explanation for—not almost everything, not most things—there is a scientific explanation for everything.

Well, after the first shock wore off I could see that Max's "great secret" had a lot going for it. First of all, it was simple. I mean gosh, if this formula really holds true at all times and in all places...well, then...holy cow. One could get a handle on things. One could depend upon the universe—depend upon it to run reliably along like a well-oiled machine. But most attractively, Max's stark brave materialism actually seemed *comforting* somehow. It narrowed the field of frightening possibilities with which one might conceivably be confronted. I still had, after all, certain childhood fears...memories of how bottomlessly black that open closet door had looked after Mommy switched off the light, of hearing for the first time about ghosts, boogie men, about hell. Yes, having a nice neat set of rules governing our place in the cosmos would make a lot of good, useful sense. Especially after dark. It's true that God would have to go...that was a bit unsettling. But come to think of it, what had he really done for me lately? I mean after all, even if God does happen to exist he's surely a bit of an absentee landlord, don't you think? How much would I really miss him?

And yet I hesitated. Max's philosophy troubled me somehow. I suppose the scientists would say that my years of brainwashing at Sunday School still shackled me. But this exciting new outlook seemed to carry a whole shipload of deeper implications that I was going to have to work out further before making any commitments.

"Max! Come up for lunch."

His mother's voice called down into the inner sanctum; the Mystery of the Ages would have to be solved some other time.

Having already eaten lunch myself, Max and I agreed that I should go out to the backyard and wait for him in his (ultra-cool) treehouse—another of my hero's many excellences. I stepped outdoors into the sunshine with my head still ringing from what I'd heard and my mind reeling with a thousand new and disturbing thoughts.

Though this was the middle of summer vacation, I remember this particular day as bright, clear, bracing, with an unaccustomed autumn-like breeze and a sharp, pure sunlight falling through the rustling green canopy overhead. I ambled absently over to the big oak which held the clubhouse aloft and started up the ladder. Looking first at my feet as I placed them carefully rung over rung, I finally lifted my head and caught a glimpse of the sky—and nearly fell out of the tree. The sky looked different. It looked...empty. I know this sounds unlikely—perhaps it sounds like a flashy metaphor dreamed up after the fact—but I swear to you that I saw it instantly, sensually, at the time, with all my ten seasoned years. Simply having this tiniest taste of how Max looked at things had altered it for me forever.

I continued soberly up the ladder and into the treehouse. What a place. An enclosed area (where Max, lucky devil, often got to spend the night) opened out onto a railed porch which looked down into a neighborhood straight out of *The Brady Bunch*. It would have been hard to get too depressed in such a setting—and so my philosophical exchange with Max simply produced in me a sort of quiet, distant daze. I remember looking vacantly out across the treetops for a while before finally searching around for something with which to pass the time.

Max kept a gigantic wooden box in this towering aerie—a box famous all over our vicinity. It was filled to overflowing with comics, baseball cards, monster magazines, and ragged *Peanuts* paperbacks; the very staff of life to kids from my generation. Though I had dipped into it many times before I dropped eagerly to the floor one more time, sliding the heavy crate up between my knees. Finally, though I didn't know it at the time, another world-shattering moment of truth had arrived. I innocently and quietly—not unlike Pandora—*opened the box.*

Right on the top of the stack was a paperback book I hadn't seen before. It was full of cartoons, very inviting, with an engaging title:

"Ripley's Believe It or Not!—2nd Series."

I'd never heard of "Ripley," whomever he might be. And as far as I knew, the supposedly famous newspaper strip it purported to be based on had never been carried in our local paper. Yet it certainly did look interesting, I had to admit...

Yes, this would do for a few minutes. It was filled with drawings of knights and conquistadors, Marie Antoinette and Henry VIII—stuff like that—and I'd already started, even at this age, to develop into something of a history bug. There was science in there, too...pictures of animals and facts about weather and planets, that sort of thing. Yet it all seemed to have a slightly different taste from what my mentor had been offering today...

And so I started reading *Ripley's Believe It or Not!* there in the summer sun, thinking it might help me forget for a while about my troubling conversation with Max.

I could not have been more wrong.

It's December 17, 1918.

It's snowing lightly outside, the sun has been down for hours. Visible through the windows of the fifth floor of the New York Globe building are the glittering lights of the great city, dolled up in Christmas lights for the holidays. The big Regulator clock on the wall reads 8:48 PM. Alice, the Chief's after hours secretary, sits at her desk doing her nails—as the door swings open violently.

"Take it, Alice."

The intruder flings onto her desk a large piece of cardboard wrapped in butcher's paper. It lands with a smack and wafts paperwork out from around it and onto the floor.

"Take it to him and tell him if he wants to fire me I'll be down the street at..."

"Down the street at the New York Athletic Club, I know. For your customary three sets of handball and half-a-dozen gin and tonics."

"Ah, and there you'd be wrong, my darling. I have a date tonight. The heavenly Beatrice Roberts is meeting me there..."

"The beauty contest winner?"

"That self same—and I sure as hell wasn't going to let one crummy cartoon louse that up."

Twenty-five year old Robert L. Ripley, regular Globe cartoonist and boy wonder of the sports pages, drops a hat onto his head and flips a loud tartan scarf around his neck. He smiles broadly, revealing more than he really intends to of the ugly buck teeth that have caused so much of his innate shyness. Since coming across from San Francisco two years ago he has perhaps overcompensated for this failing; his elaborate attempts to become known as a natty dresser are famously hampered by a complete and equally famous lack of taste.

"So you did come up with something then?" Alice asks, trying to peek under the wrapping without actually opening the package.

"Yes, believe it or not. I finally just cribbed something together out of my old files. It's the silliest, drippiest thing ever drawn but you can tell the Old Man from me that if he doesn't like it he can..." Ripley hesitates. "...well, I won't say with a lady present."

Alice smiles, pleased to be called a lady in the hard-boiled New York newspaper business.

"I can't help it, Alice. I swear that today was the slowest news day in the history of sports. I came this close to drawing an action packed panel of Babe Ruth eating Christmas pudding with his mother in New Rochelle."

"Very visual."

"You said it. What time is it?"

He looks across at the clock.

"Holy Moses. What am I doing here? Anyhow, I'm leaving! I'm out the door already..."

"Well, bon voyage…"

"I feel like I've just been let out of Sing Sing."

"Am I that bad, Rip?" Alice asks. The look on her face broadly hints that she might be willing to pinch hit if Beatrice Roberts washes out.

"Oh, you know what I mean," Ripley finishes, failing to notice. He turns and strides out the door. A few steps down the hall he calls out one last time.

"I may or may not be back tomorrow."

Alice sighs quietly and goes back to her nails.

"Ripley!"

"Uh oh..."

"Ripley, come in here."

With an unpleasant buzz, the intercom gurgles out a summons from the office of Walter St. Denis, sports editor of the New York Globe. "I want to talk to you about this damn cartoon!"

Rip carefully puts his brush back into the inkwell. He feels a lump forming in his throat as he rises to his feet. Oh well. Look at the bright side. I'll be back in Santa Rosa in time for Christmas.

A moment or two later Ripley is standing in front of his boss, thoroughly expecting to receive the pink slip. St. Denis, a little round man with watery blue eyes and tousled iron-gray hair, rubs his chin while holding yesterday's hasty Ripley cartoon with both hands.

"Rip, where the hell did you ever get the idea for this screwy cartoon you submitted yesterday?"

"I know, boss...I just...well, to tell you the truth I..."

"Phone hasn't stopped ringing since we ran the doggone thing this morning. Everybody's talking about it."

"They are?"

"What was it you called it?"

"...uh, Champs & Chumps..."

"Yeah, that was it. That stinks."

"I know."

"We used your other idea."

"My other...?"

"Yeah. Alice said you suggested it anyhow. Believe It or Not."

"Believe It or Not." Rip repeats the title slowly, still not quite sure that he's still employed.

"Anyhow, the darn thing's a hit."

"It is?"

"Going over like a house afire. Where'd you ever get an idea like that?"

"I dunno. I went through my files. It was a load of odd sports facts that I'd saved up over the last couple of years."

"You mean this stuff's really on the level? You didn't make any of it up?"

"No, of course not. What'd be the point of that?"

"You mean a guy really ran the 100-yard dash in 14 seconds—backwards?"

"Yeah, a guy in Canada did it. Forrester was the name. I've got the clipping out of a Toronto paper if you want to see it."

"You don't say. And the guy that stayed underwater six and a half minutes?"

"Paliquen—a Frenchman. 1912."

The Chief looks genuinely amazed for just an instant—then quickly throws up his poker face again.

"Look Ripley. I don't suppose you could do another one of these, could you?"

"Another one?"

"Yeah. Another Believe It or Not, I mean."

"Gee whiz, I never thought..."

"Is there enough material?"

It was a fateful question: Is there enough material? Is there—in this civilized, tamed, scientifically-explained, thoroughly-modern world of ours—enough material for one more newspaper cartoon of incredible facts and curiously unexplained happenings?

Rip himself is skeptical. After all, it'd taken him three or four years to gather the items in the first one. And how much of this sort of thing could there be, anyway? Yet Ripley knows that in this business when you find yourself with a stunt that sells papers you don't drop it until you're absolutely certain that you've squeezed it bone dry. Maybe, just maybe, with a little luck and a couple of afternoons down at the public library, he could milk this Believe It or Not! thing for a week or two, maybe a month even, before the material runs out...before he reaches the end of the world's oddities, before science de-mystifies the final mystery, before he digs up the last curiosity under the sun...

"Is there enough material?" With this little question—and without asking his permission—Fate singles out Robert Leroy Ripley, the buck-toothed bush-leaguer from Santa Rosa, California, for his weird and lonely destiny.

A year or so after my soul-shaking encounter at Max's treehouse, my parents took me on a visit to Gatlinburg, Tennessee—the great beating heart of Roadside America. Gatlinburg lies just outside the gate to America's most visited National Park, Great Smoky Mountains, where the archangel bearing the Park Service's flaming sword stands ever vigilant to keep a thousand wax museums, haunted houses, candy factories, T-shirt shops, and Elvis shrines out of God's paradise. I remember vividly what a shocking contrast there was between the cool, green stillness just inside those gates and the riot of Coney Island commerce just outside them. Yet while I still love the unspoiled wilderness there in the mountains of East Tennessee, I cheerfully confess that the magnificent neon cheesiness of Gatlinburg hit me at just the right moment to inspire lifelong devotion as well.

A warm summery night in Gatlinburg is a thing of beauty and a joy forever. Snuggled in a narrow, fragrant Tennessee valley "The Parkway" (as they call the stretch of U.S. 441 that becomes Gatlinburg's main drag) winds like an electric ribbon along the banks of the Little Pigeon River, presenting to the visitor five miles of the corniest, most concentrated Americana on the planet. On this particular evening my little family joined the hundreds upon hundreds of other tourists who wander eagerly up this magic strip every night, taking in the multi-colored sights, enjoying the aroma of fresh fudge/grilling steaks/mountain air/muscle-car exhaust that exists in just this precise proportion nowhere else, listening to the alternating soundtrack of Conway Twitty/Doobie Brothers coming out of the "cruising" cars, and scanning the way ahead for the next dinosaur-packed goofy golf course. I was deeply engrossed in this delightful pastime when my father nudged my shoulder sharply and pointed to something up ahead.

"Hey, what's this?"

Right ahead one of the Parkway storefronts seemed a little brighter than all the others. Open to the street, it had a large, cheerful lobby done up in circus colors—but what instantly caught my attention (in fact, it caught my breath) was the lobby's centerpiece. Standing in the middle of this open entrance foyer was a huge wooden barrel into which was pouring a fat, solid column of water rushing out of a big brass faucet. The trouble was, the faucet was *hanging in mid-air*, entirely unsupported or unconnected to anything, as far as I could make out. I did a whopping double-take when I saw it, I'm sure. I walked all around it, looking at it from all sides, until I was absolutely certain there were no wires holding it up or pipes feeding it in any way. I still can feel my almost physical amazement—that wonderful sensation that only the very best of magic tricks can create I literally could not believe my eyes. But there it was nevertheless...*believe it or not!*

What was this place? Stepping back out onto the sidewalk, I read the huge lighted facade that faced the Parkway and welcomed the world:

Ripley's Believe It or Not! Museum.

Instantly, I was back in Max's treehouse, still woozy from my first tincture of modern reductionism, and now gasping at my first taste of an antidote...

"Lindbergh was the 67th man to fly non-stop across the Atlantic..."

"Charles Charlesworth, of Staffordshire, England, died of old age before his seventh birthday..."

"In early 1928, a steamship captain officially reported that his ship had encountered a violent sandstorm in the middle of the Atlantic Ocean..."

"All the people on earth, working day and night for a million years, could not arrange five lettered children's blocks in all the possible combinations..."

"During a terrific tornado in Van Meter, Iowa, a full-grown rooster was sucked into a two-gallon glass jug without injury..."

Max's paperback book had taken me by the shirt collar and slapped my face. Coming right on the heels of my stern lecture about the sacred necessity of pure skepticism...well, it would have been hard to miss the irony.

"Elijah the Gaon, Chief Rabbi of Lithuania, possessed such a prodigious memory that he never forgot a book once he read it. He knew by heart the Bible, Midrash, Mekilta, Sifre Tosefta, Seder Olam, the Zohar, the Code, Rashi, Rambam, etc. and could accurately quote any passage at will."

"Seven years ago a farmer in Iowa hung his vest on a fence in the barnyard. A calf chewed up a pocket of the vest in which there was a gold watch. Last week the animal, now a staid old milk cow, was butchered for beef and the timepiece was found in such a position between the lungs of the cow that respiration--the closing in and filling up of the lungs--kept the stem-winder wound up, and the watch had lost less than four minutes in seven years."

"Frank Tower, an oiler, swam away from three of history's most famous sea disasters--the Titanic in 1912, the Empress of Ireland in 1914, and the Lusitania in 1915."

Page after page of this kind of stuff. I sat among the trees for at least an hour inputting impossibilities. There were real-life cyclops, men who walked on hot coals, true-life ghost stories, authenticated miracles, 200 year-old men, 6 year-old mothers, pitchers-of-no-hitters who lost the game, headless horsemen, fish that climb trees, unbelievably cruel emperors, unbelievably holy saints, unbelievably weird oriental customs, corpses who lead armies into battle, battles fought over sneezes, sneezes that kill people, people who eat people, people who eat a side of beef at a sitting, the shortest, the tallest, the fattest, the thinnest, the oldest, the newest, the most astonishing, the most jaw-dropping, the most calculated to inspire ten year-olds to throw up their hands and renounce simplistic philosophies forever.

"Giulio Bardi, an Italian deep sea diver, whose brother and sister-in-law had vanished mysteriously, stumbled on their bodies by chance while searching for gold five years later in a ship lying at the bottom of the sea off the Canary Islands! Moreover, the woman had a dagger embedded in her chest--and no explanation for the crime was ever discovered."

Don't get me wrong. I wasn't naive enough (even at ten) to believe that a 69 cent paperback full of cartoons was a conclusive refutation of Max's modern materialist paradigm. No, looking back I can see that Mr. Ripley's discoveries worked on my *instincts* rather than my intellect—the actual effect of his book was not so much to disprove a dogma as it was to break a spell.

"In the strangest gunfight of the Old West, Marshall Jeff Packard of Bakersfield, California, and a fugitive named 'Outlaw' McKinney drew and fired simultaneously--and each bullet entered and plugged the other man's gun!"

Then as now, I didn't doubt that taken one a time some sort of scientific explanation could be found for even the oddest of Ripley's oddities. But apparently they didn't come one at a time; they came by the book-full; they fell over one another clamoring for your attention; they had supported a daily newspaper strip since 1918. In other words, their very multiplicity began to constitute and argument in itself.

"The sailing ship 'Dundee Star,' abandoned by its crew off Midway Island, drifted completely around the earth in four years before finally piling up in 1891...on Midway Island, the very spot from which she started her phantom voyage!"

I like to think that being introduced, in the space of about two hours, to a real live atheist who preaches that everything is a machine and ain't it grand?—and then to a comic strip history book that made the entire human pageant look like nothing so much as one big issue of Weekly World News *("Woman gives birth to litter of 12!--Satan's face appears over Mt. Pinatubo")*—well, I like to think that such an experience would have rattled minds considerably older and wiser than mine. But at the time, my chief emotion was one of...exhilaration. And I came down out of Max's treehouse into a whole new world.

Ripley's Believe It or Not! had made—and still makes—me feel alive.

Obviously, I had to go in. Here was my treehouse experience made flesh, here in Gatlinburg, Tennessee.

I think my Dad paid my $2.00 admission. Then he and Mom (not being inclined toward this sort of thing) took up a spot on a bench outside and sent their eleven year-old Marco Polo off on his voyage of discovery.

For the purposes of this memoir, two galleries in this Gatlinburg museum stand out as the ones that messed me up for life:

The first was a section devoted to the founder of the *Believe It or Not!* feast himself, one Robert L. Ripley. It was here that I learned almost everything I was to know about the man for the next twenty years. He stood, as I recall, welcoming us visitors with a broad buck-toothed smile and a twinkle in his eyes that seemed to say "I am about to blow your minds, children." (I say "he stood"—actually "he" was the first of a whole waxworks-full of BION characters to be met at the museum). Though a full decade before Lucas & Spielberg put Indiana Jones on the screen, this flashy biographical display made the mild-looking newspaper cartoonist look like the flesh and blood incarnation of Hollywood's whip-slinging globetrotter. Vintage photographs on the walls told the story, recording Leroy Ripley's incalculable transformation from homely hometown baseball hero into Bob "Believe It or Not!" Ripley, international celebrity, radio star, and fearless world-renowned adventurer. Here (in classic newsreel footage) we see him pushing a frozen thirties motorcar over a Himalayan mountain pass. Now (dressed in his trademark Jungle Jim pith-helmet) we watch as he enthusiastically pumps the arm of a genuine Fiji cannibal whose gleaming white teeth are filed to razor-points.

Seems Leroy Ripley, lately of Santa Rosa, California, draws his little throwaway cartoon of a lost December afternoon and then quickly finds himself one of the great fads of the early twentieth century. Fifteen years later—fifteen years after wondering whether his "Champs & Chumps" gimmick can be milked for another fifteen days—Robert L. Ripley had traveled over 500,000 miles without a day's vacation, and had never yet failed to produce a *Believe It or Not!* cartoon every single day. By 1933, his syndicated feature was published in 30 nations, in 12 languages, in nearly 100 different newspapers in the United States and Canada. Its daily circulation was estimated at 19,712,000. At the height of the Great Depression, Robert Leroy Ripley reported an annual income of half a million dollars.

Yet I think the aspect of this gallery that impressed me most was a huge mountain of mail crammed into one of the large display cases; all of it addressed to Ripley. It seems that though he visited nearly 200 countries in search of his amazing curiosities, the best source of "Believe It or Nots" was always *the Ripley Mailbag*. The feature began with Rip's anxious question: Is there enough material? His twenty millions of readers, as it happens, answered the question by post every single day. The material poured into his office in a never-ending avalanche; in one 14-day period during 1930 Ripley received, from all over the world, *two and a half million letters*. Ripley and his staff nearly drowned in submissions. Authors Mark Sloan, Roger Manley, and Michelle Van Parys, while researching their book "Dear Mr. Ripley," recently spent days poring through the Ripley Archives, final resting place of much of this mass of unsolicited oddity. Their experience says much about the little question that sent Mr. Ripley on his mind-bending quest:

"We saw so much weirdness, so many odd things in such a compressed time, that the commonplace now seemed the exception. We'd wonder, 'Why is it that when we crack an egg to make breakfast, there's only one yolk inside?' We'd come to feel shortchanged with any egg in the Ripley Archives that had only two yolks. So many armless guitar players turned up in the files that we began to marvel at anyone who strummed an instrument with mere hands. 'What's wrong with that guy?' we'd find ourselves asking...Ripley fans sent in enough photos of pocket-watches found inside beef hearts, missing diamond rings discovered inside eggs, and lost keys turned up inside Irish potatoes to set up an improbable lost & found office. But these were run of the mill Ripley correspondence and we rarely set them aside. However, when Clinton Blume went swimming at Manhattan Beach in Brooklyn and bumped into his own monogrammed hairbrush floating in the surf—a hairbrush lost at sea when his ship was sunk by a German U-boat in 1918—now *that* was worth a pause..."

This vision of the world—the disquieting notion that one has only to print a call for oddities in the newspapers to discover that about every third person on the planet has seen a ghost, or once caught a fish wearing eyeglasses, or owns a two-headed calf—this vision uncovered in Ripley's mailbox impressed me most of all. You might say it lodged in my brain and took root. I began to wonder if this little cartoon hadn't done, in spite of itself, something rather important. In searching for his "material" Bob Ripley seemed to have inadvertently created a great engine for uncovering data about the true nature of things; a sort of alternative approach to the scientific method, if you will. As I reviewed his results a sort of "oddity principle" began to suggest itself. Consider this: if miracles happen to only one person in a million each day, then the vast majority of the world's five billion occupants will never experience one...yet they still happen *5,000 times a day*. More than enough to keep a newspaper strip in business. I guess I still didn't know philosophically whether there really is "a scientific explanation for everything." But this I did know: if even ten per cent of the things solemnly recorded by this Mr. Robert Ripley did really turn out to be true, then just that ten per cent was enough to muck up Max's spotless squeaky-clean system. Grant the ten per cent and you've already compromised the modernist world-view so badly that there really remains no good reason to doubt the other ninety.

The other gallery that stands sharp in my memory was a sort of "grab-bag" room. This section seemed to house odds & ends that didn't quite fit in elsewhere in the display; I recall that Ripley's collection of sword-cane walking sticks was shown there. The reason I remember this room so well however, was that it contained what was, for me, Ripley's most haunting exhibit. Well before you entered the room itself you heard it—laughter, continuous convulsive laughter. The source was a wax figure of a man, dressed in the garb of an 18th century French nobleman, shown grasping his stomach and bent over backwards in hysterics. The true story behind this figure (I've since forgotten the actual name and dates) told of a celebrated Paris humorist who, while writing a joke book, came up with a quip or yarn or riddle so funny that it completely paralyzed its author with laughter. I still remember word for word the punch line given on the exhibit's legend: "He laughed uninterruptedly for *eight days* without stopping to eat, drink, or sleep, before finally dying of exhaustion on the ninth day—*without having told the joke to anyone!* Believe It or Not!"

This wax Frenchman, who seemed to have stumbled into a little corner of the universe from which no one gets out alive, has stood in my imagination ever since as a fitting symbol for Robert Ripley himself. It should be very plain that something weird happened to our hero somewhere along the way. Ten years or so sufficed to turn our introverted tombstone polisher into a man who collects mummies and magical charms, who lives in a castle with six oriental concubines, who owns a large fleet of automobiles but is afraid to drive, who refuses to use the telephone for fear of being electrocuted. I began to wonder: did the newspaper cartoon that made Ripley's fortune also drive him mad? Not mad in some broad theatrical style, mind you...just quietly but radically *expanded*. "Mind expansion" was a concept much in vogue when I first toured Ripley's museum but it did seem to offer some interesting parallels. Like the fifties mouseketeers who somehow evolved into the acid-heads of the 1960's, Rip just seemed to have taken that left turn back at Albuquerque. True, the flower children took their trips with psychedelic drugs; Ripley made his by China Clipper, aboard steamers, on the backs of camels. But the results were markedly similar. The hippies came out of their reveries so altered as to be unable to interface with the existing society anymore. Rip too wore funny clothes (his favorite costume when entertaining—the scarlet robes of a Chinese warlord), seemed a little indifferent to ordinary ideas of good and evil (recall that harem...), made up his own lifestyle, and just generally seemed to have lost all interest in fulfilling the polite norms of society. He seemed in every way to be, in the words of the old hippie ballad, "traveling to the beat of a different drum." And so I finally began to wonder if Rip hadn't worn that pith helmet of his into the one place that enthusiasm and thirties "pep" couldn't get him out of. Perhaps the truth he discovered is like the wax nobleman's delightful but deadly joke; if we ever caught a glimpse of the universe as it really is we might never get over it. As they say, one does not look at the face of the Gorgon and live. After a few of these visits to Ripley's museum (and I made many return trips during the '70s and '80s) I began to suspect that Ripley's chosen vocation—to search out the odd, the incredible, the inexplicable and uncategorizable until you get to the end of the material—perhaps this was a task no man can undertake. The joke is just too funny—and even a flash of the actual truth is too much for flesh to bear. Perhaps only God's mind is strong enough to bear the burden, large enough to know the creation as it really is, and only He can ever know the heights and the depths and the unsearchable riches. Anyone else who ventures to open Mr. Ripley's daily mailbag (a continuing real-life job, by the way, which I've never envied anyone) must do so soberly, cautiously, with fear and trembling.

Which brings us back to God...and Max.

Max never did make an atheist of me. And it was his own fault, too, for leaving that Ripley paperback lying around where I could find it. Of course, I don't mean to suggest that Ripley's cartoons ought to be included in books of religious apologetics, nestled somewhere between Anselm's ontology and Pascal's wager. In fact, Ripley himself seems never to have gotten past a sort of radical agnosticism...not just about God but about everything. One of the very few glimpses available anywhere into just what kind of "unified field theory" the man himself may have entertained comes in the introduction to the original *Believe It or Not!* hardback, first published in 1929. In it, he offers the following brief thought to the disappointed millions:

This world is all a fleeting show,
For man's illusion given.

I myself ventured a little beyond this.

It seems to me that one of the things that keeps most people from embracing the religious view of reality—particularly western people from embracing orthodox Christianity—is that it all just sounds too weird to be true; angels, devils, heaven, hell, men swallowed by whales, a virgin born Savior rising from the dead. But Robert Ripley taught me that the universe itself is weird...and in just that sort of way. Even the ordinary world I already believe in turns out to be strange on close inspection...very strange...and stranger than you think.

And therefore it only stands to reason that a strange world should have a strange explanation...a strange religion.

Ripley taught me that this strangeness (odd as it may seem) is the distinctive tang of reality. You might say that *Believe It or Not!* innoculated me against Max's materialism. It taught me that if one finds a worldview (a philosophy, a religion, any general outlook on things) that *doesn't* sound weird...it's probably a comforting oversimplification. If it doesn't have room in it for the double-eyed man, for "Coghlan's Coffin," for poor little Charles Charlesworth and the true-life Mother Goose...then look somewhere else. If it's neat, tidy, overarching, and all-encompassing...it was invented by someone running from the truth, not by someone looking for it.

Ripley's Gatlinburg museum burned to the ground in 1992; fire officials blamed a faulty light fixture in the gift shop downstairs. Many of Rip's most prized possessions went up in the conflagration; favorite Chinese artifacts, personal items from his BION mansion, a hand-carved mahogany throne presented to him in 1936 by Mahatma Gandhi. But in my mind's eye I see the laughing Frenchman, giggling while Rome burns, face streaming with tears, and being slowly reduced to a sizzling puddle of beeswax on the floor. In my fancy his eternal laugh track—the voice of Robert Ripley's own destiny—was the last thing to go. In my imagination I hear that hidden tape player sputtering to a stop only as the last smoldering stick of Ripley's museum—the symbol of his life's attempt to get to the end of the material—falls into a gigantic heap of charcoal and ash.

The cheap little frame house comes down quickly. The old lady who'd owned the place since the 1880's died a few years back. Since then, the dust has settled, the paint has begun to peel, and the windows have come out behind rocks hurled by local kids. A developer bought the land recently for manufactured tract homes—the latest "progressive" thing in this streamlined year on 1940—and a contractor has sent Bud Weiss over to pull it down with his bulldozer. Half an hour's work later, Bud wipes his brow in the California sun, spreads a box lunch across what had been the front steps, and settles down with a ham sandwich in the middle of a forest of splintered beams and a hill of scrambled red bricks.

Now that the dozer is switched off the air is thick and still. But soon a big black automobile turns onto the old street; a fine expensive car that gets Bud's attention right away. It rolls slowly up to the still-standing mailbox at the end of the walk and then comes to a stop. The windows are darkened and Bud cannot see inside. It idles quietly for a full minute.

Then, a window comes down.

"You're Bud Weiss, aren't you?"

"Yeah, that's me. Who wants to know?"

"Have you learned how to catch a good hard sinker yet?"

Bud squints against the sun, trying to make out the face of the man inside the shadowed passenger compartment.

"How's that?"

"Baseball...you know."

"Who...waitasecond..."

The face, though wider, balder, and older than he remembered...

"Rip! Leroy Ripley!"

The big working man springs to his feet and rushes forward. The rear door of the car opens and then the two old friends share an energetic handshake. There are, of course, the customary politenesses; how are you, how's the wife, how you getting along, gee, but it's been a long time. But then the true past rushes up fresh in their minds. After all, the very air of Santa Rosa smells like baseball...and Bud had been Ripley's favorite catcher throughout his career with the Santa Rosa club. A guy just doesn't forget his favorite catcher...

"My gosh, I never thought I'd see you again. You're a big radio star! What are you doing back in this podunk burg?"

"You just tore down my house, you sonofabitch!"

Ripley is grinning—not really angry—but there is a serious edge in his voice.

"Your house...?"

"This is the house I grew up in. I was born here!"

Rip looks out over the rubble.

"God, what a mess."

Stepping away from the car, Ripley comes out into full view; sharp expensive pinstripe suit with a wide lapel, loud ridiculous tie from Niagara Falls, and pure white spats around his ankles...spats being already quite obsolete.

"Not a hell of a lot left, is there?" The cartoonist walks out onto the heap of rubble and begins poking around.

"Gee, I'm sorry Rip. If you'd been here an hour ago you could have seen it in one piece."

Ripley stops now and then, bends over to pick up a doorknob, a piece of glass, some little bit of junk.

"Well anyhow, Mr. Bigshot, what are you doing out here?"

"Oh, you know...traveling. Catching the China Star out of Frisco this afternoon, headed for Singapore. Heard the old place had been sold and thought I'd meet the new owner. Ha."

Singapore. He might as well have said the Moon. Bud gets along on $18 a week. Just the trip to San Francisco would be a big event on $18 a week.

"Singapore, huh?"

"Yeah. After that I guess it's...oh, what?...Burma, French Indochina, Siam...hell, I can't remember them all. Big trip anyhow."

Bud notices that along with a paid driver there is a woman still sitting in the car—alone in the back seat with a distant look on her face. Pretty woman. Bud becomes aware that he has seen her somewhere before.

"So Bud...you still play any ball?"

He doesn't. It's the commonest minor tragedy in America—somewhere along the way the sunny tousled schoolboy came to terms with the fact that he never was going to get to the World Series. Like most of us, Bud has settled down into a pleasant, comfortable life not entirely of his own choosing. Now Ripley, on the other hand—Rip had gotten close. Closer than anyone Bud had ever known, anyways.

"I guess they still talk about me around here, uh?"

"What, are you kidding? With your face on the movie screens and your pictures in the funny papers every day?"

"No, I mean baseball. I guess I'm about the biggest wash-out that ever came out of this place..."

"Wash-out? What are you talking about?"

"You know. 'The guy who broke his pitching arm playing in his first professional game.' They talked about it in the papers for weeks. And I guess they knew what they were talking about, too. Wing hasn't been worth a damn since."

Bud struggled to realize what he was hearing. Could this fellow—one of the richest men in the country from what he had heard—really be serious? Could the 'Modern

Marco Polo," the country's most eligible bachelor, star of stage, screen, and radio...could he really be mourning still over a lost stint in baseball?

The woman in the car is a movie actress. Bud is sure of it now. He's seen her down at the Paramount a thousand times, in the corny tearjerkers his wife insists on every Saturday night. She seems to be doing her nails; at any rate, she pays neither himself nor Ripley the slightest attention.

Rip piddles around in the rubble another ten minutes or so. He never mentions baseball again, but the two of them do go on to talk over old times a bit; girls they dated, fellas they've lost track of, etc. Nothing at all remarkable—until the famous cartoonist looks at his watch and decides the time has come to be on his way. At this point, Leroy Ripley waves his old teammate over to one particular bit of rubbish on the top of the heap.

"Do me a favor, would you Bud?"

"What's that?"

"Could you...would you mind taking a minute to load this into the trunk of the car for me?"

"Whatcha got?"

"Oh, I'd just like to...I don't want to mess the suit up, see? Could you just load this up? I'll pay you a little something if you don't mind doing it."

Bud steps up onto the pile. Looking down, he sees that the object selected is nothing more than an old wooden door from the front of the house. He has no particular comment about the request. Ripley helps a bit and soon the slab has been carried easily over to the car. Bud retrieves a bit of twine out of his tool kit. In five more minutes the trunk lid is tied down and the whitewashed piece of oak is sticking out of the back of the vehicle in the surfboard style that will become so familiar here in California after another twenty years or so. When the job is done Ripley discreetly shoves something into the pocket of Bud's overalls.

It is only after Ripley has said his goodbyes and stepped back into the car that Bud realizes what the door signifies. Looking down, he sees a long row of notches and numbers pencilled along one edge: Dec. 24, 1899 - 4'2"--Apr. 11, 1902 - 4'10"--June 23, 1905 - 5'6" It's the front door of Ripley's boyhood home—and his mother has used the edge of it to carefully record her little fellow's progress toward manhood. The last entry is Sep. 6, 1909. After that the numbers disappear. Mother's young man goes off to find his own destiny.

The old door swings out from under Bud's nose as the big black car rumbles slowly off to Singapore. Bringing the tight little wad out of his pocket, he sees that it is a new fifty dollar bill.

Bud never hears from Leroy again until May 27, 1949, when he reads—along with the rest of the world—that Robert "Believe It or Not!" Ripley has died of heart failure at his vacation home in Florida.

A few years back (about the time I started gathering material for this piece) the spirit of Robert Ripley came to me again.

I'd been sojourning in Southern California and, not unlike the thousands of other aspiring writers and filmmakers who come looking for *Hollywood!* and find Hollywood instead, I ended up selling shoes. Literally selling shoes at a big discount store in Reseda. I gather that back in the 1930's when Bing Crosby was crooning about it, the San Fernando Valley was a pretty wonderful place to live. When I got there in the mid-eighties however, it had already decayed, under the influences of smog, strip malls, and freeway gridlock, into a queasy cross between *Dragnet* and *Mad Max*; the place where 95% of the nation's hard-core pornography is made. I'll be honest, it started getting to me. Every day I stayed there that cloudless California sky looked more and more empty...like the one at the top of Max's treehouse ladder. I finally decided that life was just too darn short and I made the decision to return to the green hills of Georgia. But unfortunately, I had bills to pay before I could go, and moving expenses to raise. And so I slogged away at Shoe City, pitting my daily commission against minimum wage and watching minimum wage win every day, slipping deeper and deeper into a smog-brown funk, a forgotten prisoner in an old *CHiPs* episode.

This particular day was getting along like all the rest...until a tall, dark-haired lady appeared at my station with an unusually specific request.

"Do you have a pair of gray eel-skin pumps in a size 7?"

Well, I must say ours was a very large shoe store—70,000 pairs we advertised, stacked to the ceiling on 12-foot racks in a cavernous back room. But I knew right away that her request was going to be a bit dicey. We had, I remembered, displayed some eel-skin pumps a few months back; they were expensive, came in a limited range of colors, and had not sold well. In fact, I was afraid they'd all been sent back to the warehouse, since as far as I knew neither I nor any other of the salesmen had even been asked about them in weeks. But I did agree to go back and check, without much real hope of success.

Wonder of wonders, there was one lonesome pair of eel-skin pumps still loitering about; they were gray, but the size was 7 1/2 rather than the specified 7. Now we salesmen (yes ladies, your suspicions are correct) were trained to try, in this situation, to get women to go ahead and buy the wrong size anyway...on the theory that there's a good chance she will keep them if the fit is anywhere within the general ballpark. So I took them forward to the dark-haired lady, intending to do my level best to get her to purchase a pair of shoes which I knew wouldn't fit.

Not surprisingly, she didn't go for it. We tried them on and they were, of course, too large. Discovering this, she rose up quickly and headed determinedly for the exit. All good salesmen (so I'd been instructed) will do anything short of throwing a body tackle to stop a customer from reaching the egress empty-handed. And so, tucking the shoe box under one arm, I tailed her all the way to the door trying to get her to look at something else...all to no avail. Apparently, it was "eel-skin pumps in a size 7 or bust," and she had decided to bust. I puppy-dogged her the length of the sales floor and then stopped at the exit, the dark-haired lady continuing briskly across the parking lot towards her car. Georgia was looking farther away than ever.

At that precise moment one of the cashiers nearby asked me to take a customer phone call. I agreed. I was handed the receiver and tried to sound pleasant in spite of myself.

"Shoe City, can I help you?"

I heard a woman's voice on the other end.

"Uh, yes. Let me ask you something. Do you have a pair of gray eel-skin pumps in a size 7 1/2?"

Silence. Then, weakly...

"Pardon me?"

"I said, do you have a pair of gray eel-skin pumps in a size 7 1/2?"

Looking back out into the parking lot, I could still see the dark-haired lady fumbling with her car keys...and not a phone in sight, here in the years before cell phones.

"You...you're not going to believe this, ma'am..."

"Yes?"

"...but it just so happens that I have *that particular pair of shoes in my hand.*"

I glanced quickly across the floor of our shoe store—the one with the 70,000 pairs of shoes—to see if one of my co-workers might be on an extension playing a joke. Nope, every one of them was accounted for and all the store phones were sitting idle. After a moment, the voice on the other end spoke again:

"Well. That's funny, isn't it?"

She sounded...amused. Then she just let the question hang there.

"Uh, yeah. I suppose it is. Should I put them aside? Will you be coming in for them?"

"No. No, thank you. I don't believe I will. Goodbye."

I don't think I ever returned that goodbye. The line simply went dead. A short, rippling chill rolled quickly up the back of my neck...and then suddenly I had the most unmistakable sensation that someplace, somewhere whomever—or whatever—I had just been talking to was having a good, old-fashioned belly laugh.

Yet before things could get too very creepy I was quietly cheered by a rather comforting thought...

You expected this.

You know this place. You've been here before.

This is Mr. Ripley's world...the one I first glimpsed in Max's treehouse, long, long ago. This is what Planet Earth is really like, though I'd only heard of it before in theory. And then suddenly, with an uneasy but genuine smile, I realized that *Believe It or Not!* had trained me for this moment all my life.

Sometimes I like to believe that this is the thing for which Mr. Ripley, God rest his soul, gave his sanity.

Thanks, Rip.

The ball slips gracefully from Leroy's fingers. It noiselessly cuts through the air and then, in less than the blink of an eye, it has popped satisfyingly into Bud Weiss' mitt. Finley's bat whistles impotently through space.

Strike Three.

And just like that, humble, goofy-looking Leroy Ripley is a hero.

The next few moments are a blur. There are perhaps three seconds of silence; Rip bows his head quietly. And then they rush forward in a mass—his teammates, his friends, barbers and grocers from the town, pretty girls out of the bleachers—and in an instant they have hoisted him onto their shoulders, into the sky, and they will carry him off the field as the band plays The Battle Cry of Freedom.

Leroy is happy, but his eyes fill with tears. Looking up, he sees the blue firmament overhead—wonderfully clear, full of heavenly light. He becomes conscious of the hundred warm hands holding him aloft; the respect, the love of his fellow creatures lifting him up, presenting their champion gratefully to the gods of baseball—a living sacrifice of thanksgiving. Tonight they will fill him with beer, shake his hand a great many times, slap his back. Today, the world seems like a thoroughly miraculous place.

And Rip feels that one day soon—perhaps very soon—he will make it to the big leagues.

Note: As you may have guessed, many of the novelistic details in this treatment of Robert Ripley's life are my own invention. However, you should know that the episodes I sketched do have a solid basis in fact. The BION manison really existed, just as I described it. The story behind the creation of "Champs & Chumps" was told and retold (with variations) by Ripley and others through the years; my fictional attempt to reconcile these various accounts seems to me not unlikely. Leroy Ripley's baseball career was very much as I've depicted it; he really did, believe it or not, break and thoroughly ruin his throwing arm while pitching his first professional game. Lastly, Rip did return to Santa Rosa and he really did take the front door of his boyhood home back with him to New York; it hung as the entrance to BION until that haunted castle was finally demolished in the early 1950's.

Ripley's broadcasting associate Joe Connally probably put it best: "Robert Ripley was his own greatest Believe It or Not!"

Originally published in *Wonder #12*, Summer 1996

JURASSIC PARK AND THE DEATH OF STOP-MOTION ANIMATION

Jurassic Park has killed the art of stop-motion animation.

With one mighty computer-generated blow Steven Spielberg's dinosaur epic has brought down the venerable special effects art form pioneered by Willis O'Brien, has left the world wondering how it ever could have sat through *King Kong* or *Mighty Joe Young*, has repudiated, negated, and positively invalidated the entire career of the technique's grand master Ray Harryhausen. *Jurassic Park*'s mighty Tyrannosaur has bellowed out his arrival...and current stop-motion practitioners Jim Danforth, Dave Allen, Phil Tippet, and company are jumping out of windows, like so many Wall Streeters on Black Tuesday. In short, stop-motion is as obsolete as gaslight, as dead as Caesar, as washed up, cast down, done in, and played out as anything ever has been.

Or so runs the new Hollywood "wisdom." The truth, as is often the case, is a little more subtle.

Of course, there's no doubt at all that the new "full-motion" dinosaur scenes in *Jurassic Park* are stunning. Almost literally stunning. And there's very little doubt that they have ushered in a new era of special effects magnificence. These computer generated images are simply the most vivid and convincing depictions of imaginary creatures that have ever appeared in any medium. For realism and authenticity—but more importantly for drama and impact—the dino-scenes in Jurassic Park are as far above those in *Valley of Gwangi* (1969) and *One Million Years B.C.* (1966) as those films are above *The Dinosaur and the Missing Link* (1917). And I say these things as a great fan of all three of those films and as a great fan of the stop-motion process in general.

In fact, I would classify myself as a huge and even undiscriminating fan of stop-motion animation. Like most other members of that ancient & royal unofficial order—The Mystic Knights of "I-saw-Sinbad/King Kong/all those skeletons-and-haven't-been-the-same-since"—I am deeply and madly and sentimentally in love with the stuff. I'm irrational about it. I like it when it's smooth (as it is in Danforth's *When Dinosaurs Ruled the Earth* and in practically all of Ray Harryhausen's work) and I like it when it's jerky (as it is in Danforth's *Jack the Giant Killer* and in practically all of Willis O'Brien's work). I like it when it adds to a good movie (as it does in *King Kong*) or when it's the only good thing in a bad movie (as it is in *Flesh Gordon* or *Crater Lake Monster*). I'm just a sucker for all of it; I like stop-motion, go-motion, Fantascope, "Three-dimensional Animation," Dynamation, Super-Dynamation, Claymation and just about every other kind of Mation. I even like Filmation's old *Land of the Lost* TV show. So when I say that *Jurassic Park* has made all of it obsolete, I say it as a friend, in the gentlest possible tones. I have come to praise stop-motion animation, not to bury it...but in all honesty I can't really say that a reverent little eulogy would be completely out of order at this point. Ray Harryhausen is still a genius. King Kong is still one of the five best movies ever made. Fifteen-year-olds will still stumble across afterschool showings of Sinbad and then save up their yard-mowing money for a second-hand movie camera with a trip-frame mechanism. All these things are still true...but the future belongs to the offspring of *Jurassic Park*.

The virtues of the stop-motion technique (to those of us who think it has any) have always been so plain, so up-front, that any defense of them seemed superfluous. Of all special effects techniques this one always seemed to come closest to pure creation, to most nearly justify the title "movie magic." "You start from nothing" says Harryhausen, "and you are creating an object you hope to convince somebody is alive." Before *Star Wars* and the age of Industrial Light & Magic, stop-motion animation already had just that glittering high-tech sparkle. No stage hands in baggy rubber suits, no alligators with fins glued on, no hand puppets or marionettes; stop-motion seemed to go straight from the designer's mind and onto film with an almost Krell-like freedom from physical instrumentalities. And what physical process was involved added to the mystique; one man, armed only with a jointed toy and a watchmaker's patience, goes into a dark room for a month and emerges with a writhing, raging monster twenty feet high. It really did seem like magic. But another distinct part of the appeal for us fans was that these magicians weren't flamboyant characters at all. No, they had just the opposite appeal; they were tinkerers, technicians...quiet, no-nonsense, "let's go downstairs to the shop and work this out" kind of guys. While other monster movie fans doted on flashy stories about iconoclastic writer/directors battling studio bosses for their "vision" or interviews with narcissistic actors ruminating on the sexual meaning behind the Dracula mythos, we stop-motion buffs were falling in love with a group of guys who seemed more like pipe-smoking next-door neighbors with fantastically well-organized workbenches in the garage...who just happen to bring monsters to life there rather than fixing lawn mowers. We met Willis O'Brien, the canny Irishman who discovered stop-motion photography while trying to devise a way to bring to life the little clay athletes he liked to sculpt (boxing remained O'Bie's first love 'til the day he died). We came to love "Uncle" Ray Harryhausen...whom God surely fashioned to be a clockmaker or a fix-it man...the most prosaic and stolid personality I've ever met, who nevertheless has pulled down from the sky some of the most poetic and startling images ever put on film. We met Pete Peterson, the blue-collar genius who surely would have been one of the giants of all time if his life hadn't been cut tragically short by a cruel illness. And we discovered young Jim Danforth, the clean-cut California kid, the Bruce Brown of special effects artists, who may just be the best animator of the bunch. Yep, to become a stop-motion fan was to join a fraternity of "regular guys" whose art was accomplished with shirtsleeves rolled up. Yet art it was, of a particularly clean and cerebral variety (if we fans had a fault it was pride...stop-motion monsters were clearly the most intellectual kind) and we loved it and the men who made it.

But there was always a great mystery in the lives of us stop-motion fanatics. If stop-motion is so obviously the thinking man's method for putting the fantastic on the screen, how come more people—even thinking men—don't use it? With this question we come to the trouble with stop-motion animation. The trouble with stop-motion animation, the reason the process has never quite been completely accepted by the Hollywood money men or even by the special effects community, is that evokes an odd or even weird response from audiences; people either love stop-motion or they loathe it. There doesn't seem to be any middle ground. Actually it's even worse than that. The fact is that when presented with a stop-motion fantasy scene, any given individual will have one of two standard reactions; your given individual will either be whisked away on a magic carpet of wonder...or he or she will give the whole thing up in disgust as they watch the moving-picture illusion itself breaking down in front of their eyes. It's strange, it's maddening, it's inexplicable, but it's a fact.

I've watched it happen. I have been present in a room where a video of *Jason and the Argonauts* was being presented to 8 or 10 ordinary, picked-at-random type folks. Now I personally think that *Jason and the Argonauts* ought to fly with any but the very thickest "let's watch *Home Alone 2* again" sort of crowd. Jason is exciting, it's thought-provoking, it's beautifully acted, cleverly scripted, well directed, and the stop-motion effects are just the greatest; they absolutely sparkle—both technically and conceptually. In fact,

Jason is probably the best all-around stop-motion film; by "all around" I mean that it's the strongest in all departments, the best one to show to stop-motion skeptics (*King Kong* is a better movie but the animation's not as accomplished). And I'm here to report that at this particular showing an audience split itself right in half. About forty minutes into the picture the first (and to many of us the best) stop-motion sequence in the show begins. The giant bronze god Talos ominously turns his colossal head towards us and then, accompanied by the tortured wail of tons of twisting bronze, he steps down from his pedestal to pursue us; stop-motion fans have always gone to pieces. My "test audience" took sides; half of them began to "ooh and ahh"; the magic carpet ride had begun. The other half began to snicker and hoot and make cracks about how far special effects have come—like they were watching an old *Flash Gordon* serial or something.

Well of course, my first instinctive reaction to hearing this sort of ridicule flung so carelessly at something I dearly love was a strong (but manfully resisted) urge to grab up some handfuls of hair and start knocking a few heads together. And I still say that *Jason and the Argonauts* is such a manifest work of art that even if you don't like it you ought to respect it. But this confusing experience—the discovery of "the incredible two-headed audience"—made a much deeper impression on me than that. The very existence of such a radically mixed audience reaction sets one to looking for a few answers.

Of course, at least part of this problem is caused by the strobing effect inherent in the stop-motion process and I used to think that animators could bring everyone into the fold by working harder to smooth it out. I've ended up wondering whether "smooth" stop-motion is even worth bothering about; the people who hate the process hate it no matter how smooth it is and those of us who like it like it whether it's smooth or not. The actual problem seems to be something much more fundamental. For example; in *7th Voyage of Sinbad*, Harryhausen's Cyclops strides out of his cave and the animation fan says "Wow!" Certainly he is *aware* of the strobing effect (Harryhausen recalls that it gave Kong and the Skull Island dinosaurs a certain "mystic quality") but he doesn't seem to mind it in the least. The stop-motion admirer is immediately caught up in the fantasy and swept away. But when the stop-motion "non-fan" watches the very same Cyclops come roaring out of the very same cave he apparently sees nothing but the strobing. Or, at any rate, the strobing is so up-front as to be the primary thing he notices; drama, staging, creature design...every supposed advantage of stop-motion is lost behind this flickering curtain of optical illusion. For people in this camp, the Cyclops is roaring out his unreality for every single second of screen time. The non-fan can tell he's not looking at ordinary live action (if you ask him what it is he doesn't like, the phrase "you can tell.." is often the best he can do) and he seems unable to get around this fact. For the non-fan, the fact that "you can tell" is a frame-by-frame give away that the animal being depicted is not real; it's "fake", "phony","fakey-looking."

Now, although we fans have always thrown up our hands in frustration when encountering this attitude and ended up mocking the non-fan's preference for Godzilla-style rubber suits or attributing it to simple lunkheadedness, I think a careful examination of his actual reaction to stop-motion reveals the existence of something more like...color-blindness or something. I know it sounds weird, but it almost seems as if some people can "see" stop-motion animation and some people can't. I've actually begun to suspect that something physiological might be the cause of this split; that maybe persistence-of-vision works differently in different people or that the rods & cones on people's retinas are spaced differently or something. Whether this is actually the case (or which of these two groups are the "color-blinded" ones) is a question I will leave to greater minds than mine. But certainly the non-fan's unwillingness to accept a stop-motion scene certainly is not simply a lack of imagination or intelligence. Yes, Dino de Laurentiis didn't want "those little puppets" in his monster movie (the 1976 *King Kong*), but then neither did Steven Spielberg (who recently listed *Gorgo* and *Godzilla* as his favorite dinosaur movies)...which brings us back to *Jurassic Park*.

Steven Spielberg's antipathy to stop-motion (or even go-motion) is apparently so great that when he first accepted the *Jurassic Park* project he actually intended to try to do the entire film with full-size robots. And remember: this is the same man who vividly recalls nearly losing his mind (and his fledgling director's career) trying to make full-size robots do anything at all for *Jaws*, the 1975 shark adventure—much less the vast and vigorous array of action described in Michael Crichton's dinosaur thriller. The director still hates the way his *Jaws* robots look (remember Michael J. Fox's quip in Spielberg's *Back to the Future Part 2*?—"The shark still looks fake."). And yet *Jurassic Park* was going to be done full-scale. Now *that* is a man with a powerful problem when it comes to the "little puppets."

To those of us who love stop-motion animation *Jurassic Park* was obviously a stop-motion project from the word go (or, come to think of it, perhaps a "go-motion" project). The very idea of trying to build a giant mechanical Tyrannosaur when traditional Harryhausen-style artistry is perfectly suitable, perfectly available, and perfectly wonderful just seems misguided and irrational and almost stubbornly stupid. (Or used to seem so anyway...Stan Winston's incredible *Jurassic* T-Rex is enough to make us take back some of the curses we heaped upon de Laurentiis for his laughable *King Kong* robot). This single fact alone expresses the trouble I've been describing better than any example I know: stop-motion fans invent movies to put animated monsters into, while Spielberg & Co. find stop-motion strobing such a stumbling block that any live-action movie monster (*Gorgo*?) is better than any animated movie monster.

So for better or for worse, whether you like this process in a fantasy film or hate it, this is the problem with stop-motion animation...a large portion of the potential audience for such a film (even imaginative people who normally like unusual pictures and ought to eat this kind of thing up) seem to be put off or alienated by this technique. One might even say they seem *immune* to it. There's no point in telling them they oughtn't to be because apparently they can't help it. And a film that features major special effects scenes that large percentages of people are immune to will necessarily go into the fight for box-office dollars with one hand tied behind its back.

We stop-motion fans used to say that producers had a "prejudice" against the technique. Maybe some of them did, but businessmen can't really afford too many prejudices. If there really exists a large and lucrative market for stop-motion films you can bet that any producer who has some sort of personal prejudice against the process will find, shall we say, the moral resources to overcome it. It's taken me a long time but I now believe the truth of the matter is that stop-motion animation has always been and remains something of a "cult" phenomenon.

Has *Jurassic Park* thrown Jim Danforth and Dave Allen out of work? I believe they themselves would tell you that they are already "out-of-work" when it comes to stop-motion animation and, in a sense, they always have been. Well, perhaps that's overstating the case—but I believe I can safely say that no one has ever built what is normally called a long and successful career entirely upon stop-motion animation. In the last ten or twelve years—say, since Danforth assisted Harryhausen with *Clash of the Titans*—the number of true "stop-motion pictures" released (that is, pictures with extensive stop-motion set pieces as opposed to films with a few quick cuts like *Dreamscape* or *The Terminator*) could be counted on two hands. Both Jim Danforth and Dave Allen make their living doing (and beautifully I might add) other types of special effects; matte paintings, miniatures, pyrotechnics, and high-speed photography. For the most part, stop-motion is not a career but a cherished private devotion for these men. These wonderful artists carefully treasure up the most marvelous and elaborate dreams for stop-motion films (projects like *The Primevals* and *Time Gate*) but they do it largely at their own expense and almost never get to see them completed. And this is something of a tradition. If I'm not mistaken even the founder of the stop-motion feast—the great Willis H. O'Brien—released, between 1925 and 1962, exactly five stop-motion features...in 37 years. An account of Mr. O'Brien's career (including as it does tantalizing titles like *Valley of the Mist*, *War Eagles*, *Gwangi* and at least a half-dozen other unrealized dream projects) makes for sour and depressing reading. His disciple Ray Harryhausen fared much better—16 films in 33 years—but this was largely because he was able to become a producer himself (with the help of his friend Charles Schneer) and thus cut the "skeptical businessman" out of the loop. And of those 16 films I believe *four* of them were hits. The point here is that stop-motion animation has supported—sort of—the careers of about six guys since 1925; a staggering thought to those of us who might have entertained dreams of making stop-motion films ourselves one day. And it's hard not to think that perhaps we were struggling to scale a higher and more treacherous peak than even we realized. If our sort of feelings about this kind of picture were at all widespread; if ordinary people saw in stop-motion what we see in it—nothing less than the possibility of almost pure creation for the screen—then stop-motion films would be as plentiful as slasher movies or (a happier example) as Westerns were in the 1950's. But obviously most people do not feel this way.

It's true that David Allen seems to have successfully cultivated something of an on-going relationship with Charles & Albert Band and their direct-to-video Full Moon/Moonbeam line. His work for them includes fine effects for *Robot Jox*, the *Puppet Master* horror series, and many others; a major set piece in Full Moon's recent *Doctor Mordrid* features a marvelous old-style dinosaur battle with a unique twist which is, in conception and execution, worthy of Harryhausen. But even a die-hard veteran like Allen now seems a little shy about the time-honored technique; the effects in the recent video movie *Prehysteria* (a stop-motion project if there ever was one) were accomplished by David Allen Productions...mainly with rod puppets. And so it seems as if Hollywood's longstanding dubiousness about stop-motion as a crowd-pleasing way to bring the fantastic to life seems to be turning from a trend into a truism—a process which seems likely to continue and even accelerate in the wake of *Jurassic Park*.

I guess what I'm saying is that while it may be true that *Jurassic Park* has killed stop-motion animation (and again, I say this as a great and sentimental friend of the process) it didn't really take much killing.

And so—now that I've largely admitted the claims of the new "stop-motion is dead" crowd, I come back around to my own personal doubts about this supposed death.

The Benedict Arnold in this tall-tale—a murder mystery about the assassination of an art form—is (former?) stop-motion animator Phil Tippett. Phil is a fine artist whose work for the screen goes back to the memorable monsters on Han Solo's chessboard in *Star Wars*. Since then Phil's career has encompassed the extensive stop-motion work in *The Empire Strikes Back*, a spectacular home-made "Bambi-with-Dinosaurs" called *Prehistoric Beast*, and includes the invention of the breakthrough (but now probably defunct) *Go-motion* innovation used prominently in 1982's *Dragonslayer* and in George Lucas' Tolkien-style fantasy *Willow*. When pre-production on *Jurassic Park* began in earnest early in 1991 Steven Spielberg was forced to reluctantly admit that, as impressive as Winston's animatronic T-Rex work was becoming, the picture was still going to have to rely on at least a few traditional animated cuts. Tippett was brought onto the picture to provide these and made, as the production moved ahead, extensive preparations for the making of a never-to-be-completed Go-motion version of *Jurassic Park*. Thus did destiny pick Captain Phil Tippett to be the man on watch when the great and mighty stop-motion ship struck its fated iceberg.

Deep into the production of *Jurassic Park*, Dennis Muren (a seven times Academy Award® winner for his work with Industrial Light & Magic) surprised himself and everyone else on *Jurassic Park* by presenting Steven Spielberg with unexpected T-Rex shots completed by computer animators Mark Dippe and Steve Williams which surpassed his and everyone elses' wildest dreams. Originally, computer animation had been considered only as a way to accomplish the elaborate Gallimimus herding scene in which the large number of animals in each shot would have made puppet animation extremely difficult. But when Spielberg saw a fully rendered and completely believable computer-generated Tyrannosaur walking around in broad daylight and not a strobe in sight he rashly and immediately made the decision to abandon the scheduled Tippett animation altogether in favor of Muren's technique. Spielberg later described the unveiling of these tests; "None of us expected that ILM would make the next quantum leap in computer graphics—at least not in time for this picture—but there it was, a living, breathing dinosaur, more real than anything Harryhausen or Phil Tippett had ever done in their careers. At the showing, Phil groaned and pretty much declared himself extinct."

Yes, the stop-motion animator is extinct...as dead as the dinosaurs.

Yet just as in the story of *Jurassic Park*, where dinosaurs prove that the reports of their extinction were greatly exaggerated, Phil Tippett was about to prove something about the so-called death of stop-motion animation.

The trouble with computer animation in the past was always a certain mechanical, coldly precise quality. The animated objects moved but they didn't live. Dennis Muren (who, by the way, is a long time friend of stop-motion (he began his career back in the 60's collaborating with Dave Allen and Jim Danforth on the now somewhat legendary stop-motion movie *Raiders of the Stone Ring*) wisely opted to keep Phil Tippett on *Jurassic Park* as a "dinosaur supervisor." He correctly reasoned that a stop-motion animator's long hands-on experience in learning frame-by-frame how an animal moves and how to put the spark of life into an inanimate fabrication might help to overcome CG animation's traditional problem with living creatures. "I thought it was important that we keep Phil involved in the project" said Muren, "to provide direction and guidance to our [computer] animators, many of whom did not really understand what a performance was...It took some convincing, because Phil did not feel at all comfortable with computers, but I managed to persuade him that his talents were indispensable."

Well, as it turns out, Phil Tippett did stay on *Jurassic Park* and as the hugely complex and perhaps overly ambitious effort progressed, his presence turned out to be anything but a mere sentimental gesture. He began by organizing classes for the fledgling computer animators, classes very similar to those Walt Disney conducted for his artists working on *Pinnochio* and *Bambi.* He took them on field trips to zoos and wild animal parks so that they could step out of the rather abstract world of computers for an afternoon and experience what animals really are and how they really look. He got them up out of their chairs and made them actually move with mimes and dancers. But he ended up making what I believe to have been the single most significant innovation in the successful bringing-to-life of *Jurassic Park*'s totally digital dinosaurs...and really, in bringing computer animation truly to life for the first time. In time-honored stop-motion style he breathed the breath of life into Spielberg's nonexistent wonders by bringing the creatures off the keyboard and taking matters *firmly in hand.* He designed what became known as the DID—or *Dinosaur Input Device*—and in so doing pulled off one of the more splendid ironies in movie history.

The DID looks for all the world exactly like an old-fashioned ball & socket stop-motion armature, straight off Willis O'Brien's tabletop. The difference is that the DID is not designed to be photographed. The joints are equipped with little encoders which allow any movement of the armature to be precisely recorded and exactly communicated to the digital "model" of the dinosaur which exists only inside the computer. But the armature itself is manipulated the old-fashioned way...by hand. In this way the "hands-off" mathematical process of computer animation was given the immediacy and intimacy enjoyed by the traditional stop-motion animator. Phil Tippett and his crew (all stop-motion veterans like Tom St. Amand) took *Jurassic Park*'s dinosaurs into their fingers and animated them just as surely as Ray Harryhausen did his Cyclops. Only this time the image was free from the limits of what can be done in foam rubber and latex on a photographed model. In a sense, the DID allowed Industrial Light & Magic's admittedly sophisticated animation computers to be linked directly to the most advanced super-computer in the known universe...the human mind.

So. What's the bottom line? What really happened there at ILM the day that stop-motion died? It's odd, it's paradoxical, but it's perfectly and undeniably true that Industrial Light & Magic killed stop-motion by (1) deciding to turn the whole project over to a stop-motion animator (2) letting him build ball & socket dinosaur armatures, and then (3) letting him animate them. As you will see in a moment, I don't mean to minimize the efforts of *Jurassic Park*'s computer wizards in any way. Yet the plain truth of this whole matter is that most of the CG animation in *Jurassic Park is* stop-motion animation; it's just photographed in a different way. The computer has not put Willis O'Brien out of business; it never can because animation is an art not a craft. The only person a computer can ever put out of business is the craftsman...an honorable profession but one whose main qualification is patience. And computers are singularly gifted with patience. If anyone has been put out of business it is Marcel Delgado—who, God rest his soul, is long past caring.

Yes, I know that the DID is probably a temporary stage in the history of computer animation; in fact, by the end of the *Jurassic Park* shoot the computer animators were finishing vivid, life-like scenes without it. Even so, these men *are* stop-motion animators. Yes, their ball & socket skeletons existed only on a CRT and yes, they moved them (one frame at a time) with a mouse instead of with their fingers. But the real animation (as opposed to the physical actions we misleadingly call animation) was going on where it always does, in exactly the same way it always has...in their heads. In the mind of an artist. That is where animation happens. That is where life comes from...from life. Never, in all the universe, have we ever found it to come from anywhere else.

So who gives a hoot whether a man actually wrestles with a physical puppet anymore? We've found a new way to do the old job. Now everyone can, or should, be able to see what we stop-motion fans saw all along. And make no mistake; it *is* the old job. Every audience that applauds *Jurassic Park* is cheering for Willis O'Brien, for Ray Harryhausen, Jim Danforth, and all the rest. These men were not sold out to any particular technical process. They were pursuing that old dream. What they were after—what kept them up all night under those hot lights swearing at a rubber & hair mannakin—was that magic, elusive, god-like dream...*pure creation*. To be able to think a thrilling thought and then send that thought winging non-stop (or perhaps with a brief lay-over as a beautiful pre-production rendering) into the minds of a receptive audience. That's a dream a man can devote a life to. *That* is what animation really is...whether your tool is a supercomputer, a rubber doll, or just a pencil.

What *Jurassic Park* has really done is to throw open to everyone the door which opened for some of us in 1925 with Willis O'Brien's *Lost World.* Because they have overcome the one technical rock of offense that kept the masses from seeing the breakthrough nearly 75 years ago, the creators of *Jurassic Park* have reaped what they did not sow, there in the summer of 1993. The theater exits opened. The audiences came out exhilerated. Their minds raced ahead into the future at the speed of thought. "If a movie can show that," they realized, "a movie can show *anything*." Pure creation. We old-fashioned stop-motion types smile—a little bemusedly, a little patiently—but we smile and are gratified. They understand. Now they can see it. We won't have to say "But can't you see?" anymore. They *do* see...and are astounded. The look on their faces is exactly the same one 13 year old Ray Harryhausen wore back in 1933, when he stepped, blinking in the California sun, out of Graumann's Chinese Theater after his first encounter with the mighty *King Kong*.

You see, Harryhausen and O'Bie, poor old Pete Peterson and the rest—far from being old-fashioned, out-of-date, antiquated...were just a little ahead of their time.

Stop-motion is dead; long live stop-motion.

Originally published in *Wonder #9,* Winter 1994

AVE MARIA GROTTO: A FIRST-HAND ACCOUNT

Someday you may find yourself at Ave Maria Grotto.

It's just east of Cullman, Alabama on Hwy. 278, about 50 miles north of Birmingham. The billboards (cryptically referring to it as "Little Jerusalem") can be seen on roadsides all across the South. Of the millions who have seen these signs, thousands of us (okay, hundreds) decided that we really did owe it to ourselves to find out what "Little Jerusalem" is doing in North Alabama and actually made the pilgrimage. When you join us—when *you* reach Ave Maria Grotto and *you* stand there goggling at it under the piney woods—you'll be glad you read this article. You'll probably laugh a lot when you get to "Little Jerusalem". You may conclude after close examination that the entire four acres fell to earth on a meteor from another planet. But if you hadn't come across this essay I think you might have missed the most curious and the most wonderful thing about Ave Maria Grotto. I'm here to see that you don't.

If you happen to be a really seasoned patron of that obscure but delightful corner of the American experience called the Roadside Tourist Attraction, you will begin your journey into "Little Jerusalem" by lingering for a moment in the ubiquitous "snow-globes & big pencils" gift shop and purchasing the official four-color circa-1960 guidebook entitled *Sermons in Stone.* This marvelously corny publication (which has defied every known law of entropy by reaching 1992 with every gushing word and every photo of admiring women in Jackie Kennedy hairdos intact) promises a treasure trove of wonders within: "*... a panorama of beauty... reproductions of European wayside shrines and miniature replicas of famous buildings and churches placed beside the wooded path which winds its way through this flower bedecked park... a cave, roofed and covered with artificial stalactites...*" It all sounds like heaven on earth to anyone who grew up begging Dad to pull that big Roadmaster wagon off the highway for an hour or two at Rock City or Santa Claus Land.

If you still have any money left after your visit to that gift shop (with its "Little Jerusalem" Viewmaster reels, etc.) you will probably want to look up from *Sermons in Stone* long enough to purchase your ticket. Somebody's grandmother—a smiling gray lady behind the ticket counter who calls you "Sugar"—points you at the entrance portal and encourages you to go right ahead and take as many pictures as you want to; the implication, of course, being that Ave Maria Grotto is so impressive that once you lay eyes on it you will be compelled, like the throngs who have gone before you, to pull out your camera and make like a Voyager spacecraft on a Jupiter fly-by. That's perfectly normal, she seems to be saying, and nothing to be ashamed of. Likewise, the freckle-faced teenager who takes your ticket at the door assures you that you can take all the time you need—it's a (with a pleasant Alabama twang) "self-guided tour". And he's pleased to see you have your copy of *Sermons in Stone* in case you have any questions. If you're anything like me, you will have plenty—but the guidebook only makes it worse.

As you step out into Ave Maria Grotto... well, I'll let the guidebook tell it. *"As the visitor catches sight of the entire layout of the park... the immensity of the undertaking is realized. The visitor is enthralled by the beauty unfolding before his eyes... It is a feeling, shared by countless thousands, that no words—however accurate and beautiful—could convey."*

Strangely enough, what the authors of the booklet seem to have missed somehow is the thing that stares most people in the face as the first and most obvious fact about Ave Maria Grotto. As a matter of fact, most modern tourists find that one very accurate word *does* suffice to express their feelings about the spectacle unfolding before their eyes...and that word is *tacky*; they find "Little Jerusalem astonishingly and stupefyingly tacky—the concrete equivalent of a 900-foot Jesus, the world's largest plastic 3D portrait of the Virgin Mary with all the pink candles blazing.

Now let me say that I'm not entirely immune to this viewpoint. "Little Jerusalem" does turn out to be a great big garden full of tinkered-together miniature scenes out of Bible stories and memorials to saints most people never heard of, made out of odd bits of junk and pieces of broken pop bottles. Over here, a six-foot Tower of Babel stands next to a replica of Noah's Ark covered with ceramic dime store farm animals. Over there, a figure of St. Scholastica stands on a pedestal made largely from empty blue cold cream jars. Let me admit from the start that the place is one-of-a-kind to say the least and I certainly won't begrudge anyone the simple pleasure of laughing good and hard for a while over finding anything so weird and unlikely out here in the Alabama woods. But unless you're very, very dense or very hip and sophisticated it will probably occur to you to stop chuckling long enough to wonder who could have have put up such a thing...and *why*.

And here's where I think this little article might be of some help. If you're clever enough to go beyond that initial shock of discovering that there certainly are people who think and act very differently than you do (a point at which laughter is perfectly legitimate, by the way), then discovering Ave Maria Grotto can be like discovering a lost civilization. It's a good rule to remember that most people who act strange have something very interesting on their minds. If you're curious enough about what that something is—if you really want to know how this weird outcropping of psychedelic piety came to be poking out of the stony southern highlands—then I've found that you can spend a very entertaining afternoon walking through "Little Jerusalem" like a detective looking clues at the scene of a crime. And you can piece together quite a story to take to the folks back home.

Let's go ahead and start walking down Ave Maria Grotto's "flower bedecked" trial. Up ahead is your first monument, a sort of free-form obelisk made out of concrete, bleached coral, and some of those green glass balls fishermen once used to keep their nets afloat. It looks like one of the Watts Towers or maybe like a signpost for UFO traffic. Saying just what it is supposed to *be* would present quite a problem if it weren't for the carefully lettered little plaque posted under it. (By the way, a cardinal rule to remember at all Roadside Wonders is to *always read the signs*; the signs are the window into the soul of your host). This one says, "This was Brother Joseph's first monument..." and then goes on to tell us about said Brother Joseph.

Joseph Zoettl was a Benedictine monk who came to America from Bavaria in 1892 and was assigned to St. Bernard Abbey near Cullman in what was then *very* rural Alabama. It was here that he developed a hobby of building miniature shrines in his spare time. *"Brother Joseph first erected the miniatures on the monastery recreation grounds. Because so many of the replicas he made were of famous sites in the Holy Land the numerous visitors who began to flock to the Abbey named it Little Jerusalem."* You see, there's one of our questions answered already. Let's read on.

"Numerous friends of St. Bernard began to send in statuary around which Brother Joseph would wield his magic in cement, stone, marbles, tiles, shells, rocks, chandelier prisms, and beads. These little items - many sent from all over the world - have been worked together to form the various shrines and replicas which number about one hundred and fifty."

These hundred and fifty shrines are undeniably impressive. Here are very detailed little re-creations of everything from St. Peter's Basilica in Rome to the Hanging Gardens of Babylon, the Alamo, San Juan Capistrano, the Tomb of Lazarus, the Parthenon, the Pantheon, and the Temple of Jerusalem...they're all here for your perusal and lots of other important places you knew nothing about until you saw them here. But the most illuminating and even unsettling thing erected in these gardens turns out to be those little placards, the legends that are meant to tell you what you're looking at.

There are dozens and dozens of these signs and someone really seems to have thought that you would want to read them all. Never mind that actually doing this—actually taking the time to carefully note what year Pope Julius II commissioned the Sistine Chapel, for example—would be a lesson in world civilization that would have you standing out here in the woods till the cows come home. Never mind; the authors of these placards seem to have unlimited faith in your interest and good will. As a matter of fact, the creator and keepers of Ave Maria Grotto are blissfully unaware that you have been laughing at them and might be laughing still. Go as far down the trail as you like; these astonishing signs continue reverently along and the authors never suspect that anyone might possibly feel anything but admiration and humility standing before a shrine to the Immaculate Conception decorated with broken bathroom tiles and cat's eye marbles. And I guess that all this innocence starts to get to you after a while. Reading these signs you start to feel like a cad—like a deserter mistakenly getting a medal for bravery or a cheating husband whose wife goes around telling everyone that mutual trust holds their marriage together. You begin to realize that these people are paying you a compliment. They are treating you like a child. That is, they are expecting you to remember enough of your childhood to see their little plot of tacky miniatures as a child would see it: as a fabulous garden of wonderful toys—which it is. Guys, if you doubt me just think for a moment how great it would be to have a G.I. Joe adventure in here!

Brother Joe studded Ave Maria Grotto with ordinary marbles like they were just as beautiful as priceless gems—and, by golly, they are! That little monk thought blue glass jars from Woolworth's are pretty—and, come to think of it, he was right! When you learn to look at it in this way—with the eyes of a five-year-old—Ave Maria Grotto starts to look pretty doggone neat. The "tackiness" has gone right out of it. Anybody can see that this place is charming, sweet, and a whole lot of fun. And here's the main clue that solves our little detective mystery, the key that unlocks this strange and "tacky" little world. Looking at Brother Joe's "Little Jerusalem" like it was a fabulous and unexpected Christmas present under your tree, you start to become aware that seeing things as "tacky" comes from the need to look around at what other people are liking and then like the same things. But Brother Joseph, like a little child, obviously launched out and followed his heart. He was not sophisticated enough to realize that most people, no matter how hard he worked, would laugh at what he was doing. And you start to see that the wonder of Ave Maria Grotto is that this man cared about what he was doing even if nobody else did. His own innocence has erupted out into these Alabama woods and if we are listening at all it will humble us.

At the end of the trail, after you've seen all one hundred and fifty shrines, a glass case has some photos of the man himself. You see Brother Joe, a rather homely and (by the end of his life, at least) quite hunchbacked little fellow with big hands, dressed in a brown habit or sometimes in some old overalls. Some of the pictures show him wearing a happy grin as he pushes an old-fashioned wheelbarrow along the very trails upon which you are now standing. Looking at these, you start to get a real and very revealing glimpse of a quiet little man who labored the better part of an 83-year life on this Alabama hillside. He seems to have shovelled coal in the Abbey's basement when he wasn't rebuilding Monte Cassino, the Fortress Antonia, or the Circus Maximus. Looking at these pictures, seeing this diminutive monk's whole life on a few old squares of yellowing paper, you may start to wonder if he wasted it here. After all, while he was shovelling his coal and working (all through the '30s, '40s, and '50s) on his castles and temples here in the dappled shade of "Little Jerusalem", free successful people in New York and Berlin were having affairs, getting divorced, completing stock mergers, and attending cocktail parties. As a matter of fact, I would say that we are faced with a choice here at "Little Jerusalem". I would venture to say that Brother Joe was either one of the stupidest people that ever lived—or one of the wisest. Come to Ave Maria Grotto and decide which.

At the conclusion of your journey through Ave Maria Grotto you will notice a rack of free brochures standing by the exit (a true devotee of Roadside Wonders will take as many of these as he or she can carry away). Your eyes scan the multi-colored tiers: *Ruby Falls, Tweetsie Railroad, Fields of the Wood, Grandfather Mountain, Christus Gardens, Storybook Land.* And then you realize the truth—there are *other* places like Ave Maria Grotto. Lots of them, all over the place. Each of them with their own "Brother Josephs", their own particular way of confronting you with startling 1940s Mom & Pop innocence.

And *confronting* really is the right word; each of these places is waiting to grab you by the shoulders and shake you until your teeth rattle - until you confess that yes, Horatio, there are more things in Roadside America than were dreamt of in my philosophy.

Originally published in *Wonder #7,* Autumn 1993

FRANKENSTEIN'S BRAIN—AND PRISON REFORM

Not long ago, the U.S. Catholic Bishops issued another of their plaintive calls, asking us to fix our "broken and destructive" criminal justice system here in America. Most of us paid this call no attention at all. Perhaps this was to be expected; I'm afraid the USCCB's recommendations have not always been free from a certain tincture of worldly wisdom and many of us have trained ourselves to take their trendier pronouncements with a grain of salt. This one, however, comes straight from the heart of the Gospel, straight from that great Prison Reformer who, on Judgment Day, will chide the condemned in these words: "I was a stranger and you did not welcome me, naked and you did not clothe me, sick and in prison and you did not visit me." [Mt 25:53]. Let's all take a moment or two, then, to reflect upon how meaningful Christian prison reform might actually be accomplished here in 21st century America.

First of all, let's concur that just tinkering with the existing mess won't do. What we're dealing with here is such a complete and total breakdown, such a ghastly human train wreck, that anything less than a strong urge to go immediately back to the drawing board reflects ignorance of the situation. What's going on now is simply a nightmare in the daylight. Our country owns nothing less than the highest *per capita* number of incarcerated persons on the planet. If every man, woman, and child living in an American prison right now were gathered up in one place, you'd have a metropolitan area the size of Milwaukee, Wisconsin.

And make no mistake—once they're in, they're in to stay. Less than fourteen percent of these people, once released, will ever succeed in becoming "useful members of society" again; they'll either go back into prison later or be added to the welfare roles as "unemployable" ex-cons.

Either way, they've become permanent wards of the state. Rehabilitation is a fairy tale—and, sadly, it's a storybook ending that most Americans don't even want for these people anymore. What *do* we want, then? I'm afraid most of us just want them to *go away*—either via the death penalty or into our ever-growing and ill-funded chain of ramshackle prisons.

Yet it's at just this point in our musings that we begin to get an intriguing glimpse of the philosophical dead-end that produced the tragedy…and a possible way out.

Remember the old Boris Karloff classic *Frankenstein*? In that film, the mad doctor's experiment goes awry because his hunchbacked assistant has stolen the wrong brain for his creation—not a healthy, normal brain but a brain from a different jar, a jar marked "abnormal," the brain, we are told, of a criminal. This is why Frankenstein's monster has turned out to be such a brute—because there's something wrong inside his head, because he has (almost literally) a screw loose someplace. His criminality is *hard wired*, so to speak—built in at the factory—and we can see that he's a lost cause right from the start.

Well, is there, in real life, any such thing as "the criminal brain"?

Not according to the teachings of the Catholic Church. The Church teaches that criminality resides in the *soul*, not in the body; and it's we ourselves who make these evil choices, not some defective organ hidden within. Of course, there are people who do suffer from mental illnesses of one kind or another, illnesses that do cause them to lose control in anti-social ways. But if they've truly lost control then they aren't really criminals in the Christian sense of the word. A man literally out of his senses can't be blamed for what he does, any more than a motorist can be blamed for wrecking his car if the steering wheel comes off in his hands. No, true criminality enters the equation only when free, self-determining souls under God, who know right from wrong, freely choose to do the one and not the other. This state, theologically speaking, is known as *sinfulness*, and the condition that created its worldwide prevalence is known as *original sin*. Ever since Adam's fall we *all* know that downward pull, we *all* experience temptation and then—when we fail to resist it—actual guilt. So in that sense, we're all like Frankenstein's monster. We all got the "criminal brain."

And since criminality is spiritual, the Church's remedies for it are likewise spiritual. In countries where the Catholic worldview has dominated, prisons haven't been called "correctional facilities" (i.e., places to repair a broken machine) but *penitentiaries*…a place for *penitents* where the object, of course, was *penance*. These were places where the guilty soul could expiate its crimes on earth, where the criminal could work off what was known (in a very valuable phrase) as "his debt to society." And once the debt was paid, the debtor was forgiven. The slate was wiped clean and absolution was dispensed.

But there never can *be* any absolution for a criminal brain. All we can hope to do in that universe is to segregate those who got one, and keep them safely away from us lucky folks who got theirs out of the other jar.

How did this mechanistic, sub-Christian outlook become so pervasive in America? Much of it, I think, can be traced to our nation's Calvinistic cultural background. Calvinism holds that God chose, from the foundation of the world, which human souls would be elect and which would be reprobate. Thus, a man's sins can't really be said to *damn his soul* so much as they reveal his soul to *have been damned* all along. Most of these American Calvinists gradually evolved, over the 18th and 19th centuries, first into Unitarians, and then finally into freethinkers and atheists. But this strong sense of determinism has clung to their outlook to this very day. In the Calvinist scheme (whether religious or secular) a man does society a *favor* by committing a crime and getting caught. He has let the cat out of the bag. He's revealed himself as one of the *broken ones*, as a man with a criminal brain, capable of criminal acts—not like the rest of us. And now he can be safely herded into the national holding pen where he won't be able to hurt anyone any more.

It seems to me then, that the solution to our prison problem lies in a renunciation of heresy. We need to stop thinking of criminals as a tribe apart, but as sinners like ourselves. Period. And what do these, our fellow sinners, need? They need to be offered *penance*, a chance to pay their debt to society. What we are currently offering them instead is the mark of Cain on their foreheads and Hester Prynne's Scarlet Letter on their breasts.

Even if a person does manage to get out of one of our "correctional facilities" without becoming a victim of homosexual rape, a certifiable basket case, or a trained professional miscreant, we have already pronounced a life sentence on them. What do I mean? I mean that these people will carry a criminal record with them forever. The debt, in other words, can never really be paid, and the slate is never wiped clean; it's too important to warn the "normal people" about their criminal brains. In a word, we have removed any effective possibility of *restoration*...and in response, our "penitentiaries" have become sinks of despair.

If, on the contrary, we were to bring back the concept of restoration in our system—by eliminating criminal records (except in the case of true psychological compulsions like serial rape or child molestation)—then our prisons could become penitentiaries again. We could begin *collecting* the debt to society, through work programs, vocational training, church attendance, personal development, and education. Rather than assigning prison terms in arbitrary numbers of years (years to be spent sitting around smoking and watching Jerry Springer) we might assign sentences in terms of *debt to be paid*—debts that might be worked off more quickly through industry and initiative, less quickly through sloth and insubordination. And the sooner the debt is paid, the sooner the absolution (which must be total) can be given.

Of course, the exact details of such a proposal would have to be carefully worked out by wise statesmen and orthodox thinkers, on the basis of what people are now calling "tough love." Business, in particular, would have to be weaned off some of their addiction to government money. That way, part of what society now pays contractors to do could be accomplished instead by those who already owe society this debt we've been talking about. There would be other difficult paradigm shifts as well. But the effort, I believe, would be well worth making.

One thing is for certain. We must never forget, even in the name of "law and order", the great prayer Jesus taught in His Sermon on the Mount: "…forgive us our trespasses, as we forgive those who trespass against us…For if you forgive men their trespasses, your heavenly Father also will forgive you; but if you do not forgive men their trespasses, neither will your Father forgive your trespasses." [Mt 6:14-15].

After all, Christ himself spent the night in jail once.

Originally published by *Catholic Exchange,* Autumn 2001

THE STARS FELL ON NEW JERSEY

Incorporating Portions of the Orson Welles "War of the Worlds" radio play written by Howard Koch

From a planetary perspective the scene that had just taken place in the little three-room house there in Hackettstown, New Jersey was, unfortunately, not a very unusual one. She told him to go to hell. He told her goodbye...and reminded her that most of his old girlfriends were still single and still interested. Then he turned and walked out the door, slamming it behind him. For a moment there was silence. Then, through an open screen window, she heard their pitiful old car rattle away into the night. The baby started to cry and then she did too.

Tom and Ruby Loudermilk had been high school sweethearts; Class of 1936. They married at 18, were made the parents of a beautiful little daughter at 19, and now, on this crisp Sunday evening of October 30, 1938, were ready to call it quits at age 20. And the sad thing was that they still loved each other. Tom was a dreamer. He worked at the local mill but what he really wanted was to be an artist. Ask anyone in town; ever since age five Tom Loudermilk had loved to draw and to make up his own comic strips and to invent wild tales about outer space like the ones in that crazy *Amazing Stories* magazine. And now it was common knowledge that Tom trudged off to the mill every night dreaming about going to work someday at the Walt Disney Studios in Burbank, California. But the plain fact was that Tom's dreams interfered with his work at the mill. Ruby said he had no ambition there and, really, she wasn't far wrong. He got passed up for every promotion and he didn't seem to really care. Before long they were getting behind on the bills. It looked like they might lose the house. And then came word that there might be some lay-offs after Christmas…

Tom loved Ruby. He really did. And she hadn't meant it...he knew that. But when she blurted out, through tears, that she sometimes wished she'd married Frank Allen (who became an engineer and took his wife to live in New York City on $12,000 a year) every bottled up ounce of suppressed anguish and panic came out. And Ruby just happened to be in the way.

"...and it is the opinion of this commentator, that, in spite of all our hopes and our prayers, this new accord this Munich agreement will not, no matter how many times and with what apparent sincerity he assures us otherwise, I repeat, will not satisfy the ambitions of Adolf Hitler. I know that many will say and have said that I am an alarmist; that the German people are simply seeking to redress some of the excesses which came in the wake of the World War. But I have read Herr Hitler's books...and I have heard his speeches. And all the world may see plainly that he continues to build the German army, even as we speak, into the greatest war machine ever created. And I tell you that this man is drunk with success. And I tell you that his government is barbaric and inhuman. And that he will never rest until all of Europe, and perhaps more, is under that government..."

Ruby wiped her nose with the sleeve of her nightgown and switched the radio station angrily. That was the last thing she needed tonight—more bad news, more frightened war talk. Tom had been gone—what was it?—a half-hour now. She was just beginning to get hold of herself, the baby had fallen asleep from sheer exhaustion, and this man on the radio wanted her to think about war. Sure, everybody knew it was coming. They've only been harping on it for five years now. Everyone was sick to death of hearing about it—or Ruby certainly was anyway. Tom was gone, out into the night—talking about his old girlfriends. No, she wouldn't think about that. He would come back. She was sure of it. But until he did she needed something on the radio to help *settle* her mind, not unsettle it further. Something ordinary. Something stupid and homey. Some music or something. Anything but war talk.

It was dark in their simple, only slightly shabby living room—except for the large green dial on the face of their big RCA set. But the glowing console lit the room well enough for this particular night; a night where the world seemed unfriendly and threatening in almost every way and Ruby only wanted to sit quietly, very quietly, as if holding perfectly still might prevent her life from unraveling any further. Even the sharp autumn breeze drifting through the window seemed only to chill and frighten. Where was that music? Ruby twisted the dial impatiently. Surely somebody was playing something cheerful tonight...

Announcer:
...for the next 24 hours not much change in temperature. A slight atmospheric disturbance of undetermined origin is reported over Nova Scotia, causing a low pressure area to move down rather rapidly over the northern states, bringing a forecast of rain, accompanied by winds of light gale force. Maximum temperature 66; minimum 48. This weather report comes to you from the Government Weather Bureau.

...We now take you to the Meridian Room in the Hotel Park Plaza in downtown New York, where you will be entertained by the music of Ramon Raquello and his orchestra.

(Spanish theme song...fades)

Tom guided the rattling, complaining old A-Model down Route 9 towards town. He had the windows open and noticed that the breeze had picked up a little. That late October smell was in the air—harvested fields, burning leaves, all the bracing outdoor smells of autumn. Still fifteen minutes or so from Hackettstown, Tom passed only the occasional car going the other way, headed toward Trenton and civilization. Toward real life. Toward real people doing real things. Things they liked and things that mattered.

Rita Daniels. She'd been Tom's best date, his favorite flame back in school…other than Ruby. Rita was sweet. She wasn't beautiful—just smart and quick, full of jokes and horseplay, wide-hipped and pretty in a broad, gum-chewing sort of way. She liked boys. She'd liked Tom especially. And she didn't ask her fellas how much they were worth before kissing them. If she liked you, she just liked you. Tom needed to feel from someone right now, like somebody could just *like* him for a little while without caring whether he'd ever amount to anything or not. He decided that Rita would be the perfect person with which to share half a bottle of gin with on a night like this. Tom mulled it over a moment; yeah, Rita was still single, still worked, he believed, at the Silver Grill, a little meat-and-three on the other side of town. It'd be open right now, in fact, lit up like a Christmas tree, filled with the Sunday night dinner crowd laughing and smoking and listening to Edgar Bergen on the radio. He pressed the accelerator a little more firmly.

Speaking of the radio, a little music would help right now. He found the dial and snapped it on...

Announcer:
Good evening ladies & gentlemen. From the Meridian Room in the Park Plaza in New York City, we bring you the music of Ramon Raquello and his orchestra. With a touch of the Spanish, Ramon Raquello leads off with "La Cumparsita."

(Piece starts playing)

Just the thing. Tom wondered if Rita still loved to dance the way she had. He remembered her as the best dancer he'd ever seen. He remembered her dancing close, intimately, smelling of rose water. Right now a dance with Rita Daniels sounded just like heaven.

Ruby sat alone in the dark. The silly Latin dance music was comforting in just the way she'd hoped it would be. Outside, at least, things continue as they always have. Everyone else, at least, is having a good time tonight; dancing, dining, drinking, marrying, and giving in marriage. The world has not come to an end after all.

She closed her eyes. The pleasant, obvious tune played long enough for her to relax a little; her head drifted back into an old cushion. She might even be able to sleep for a moment. Yes, that sounded nice. A little nap. And then, when she woke up, perhaps Tom would be back.

Ruby barely noticed when the dance music was interrupted by another announcer's voice...

Announcer #2:
Ladies and gentlemen, we interrupt our program of dance music to bring you a special bulletin from the International Radio News...

Oh no. Not more war news, surely...

Announcer #2:
...At twenty minutes before eight, central time, Professor Farrell of the Mount Jennings Observatory, Chicago, Illinois, reports observing several explosions of incandescent gas, occurring at regular intervals on the planet Mars.

The spectroscope indicates the gas to be hydrogen and moving towards the earth with enormous velocity. Professor Pierson of the observatory at Princeton confirms Farrell's observation, and describes the phenomenon as (quote) like a jet of blue flame shot from a gun (unquote). We now return you to the music of Ramon Raquello, playing for you in the meridian Room of the Park Plaza Hotel, situated in downtown New York.
(Music plays for a few moments until piece ends...sound of applause)

Mars. A zillion miles away. Why do they bother to report news from a zillion miles away? Well, at least it wasn't more about the war; any news that doesn't have Hitler in it is good news. The report made her think of Tom again. It was the sort of thing Tom would be interested in. Mars, Jupiter, Outer Space—right up Tom's alley.

Announcer:
Now a tune that never loses favor, the ever popular "Star Dust." Ramon Raquello and his orchestra...
(Music)

Tom turned the volume back down. Explosions on Mars. Like a flame shot out of a gun, they said. That was mighty odd. Like something out of one of his magazines. Could be volcanoes, he supposed. A volcano blast might look like that. Gosh, but that's a weird thing to hear about, though.

He pulled quietly up to the Hwy. 73 junction, stopping at the red light there—still 2 or 3 miles from town. While waiting for the light to turn, he noticed how quiet the evening was. His was the only car in sight. Old Man Henning's PURE Station was closed Sundays and sat there dark and still. A cool breeze pushed some fallen oak leaves across the road. The traffic light swung a little in it, before finally flashing green.

Announcer #2:
Ladies and gentlemen, following on the news given in our bulletin a moment ago, the Government Meteorological Bureau has requested the large observatories of the country to keep an astronomical watch on any further disturbances occurring on the planet Mars. Due to the unusual nature of this occurrence, we have arranged an interview with the noted astronomer, Professor Pierson, who will give us his views on this event. In a few moments we will take you to Princeton Observatory at Princeton, New Jersey. We return you until then to the music of Ramon Raquello and his orchestra.
(Music...)

Ruby knew just what Tom would do if he were home. He'd scramble up into the attic and bring down that old telescope. Then he'd stay out in the yard all night and try to get her to do the same. And he'd make her bend over and squint up at some fuzzy dot in the sky and talk to her for hours about galaxies and comets and meteoroids. Suddenly her throat got tight and her eyes filled up with tears again. She didn't...couldn't begrudge him his dreams. She never had. She loved his boyishness, his silly enthusiasms. They were the very essence of what she loved. It was only that she could see what was coming so clearly. The Bank doesn't care how boyish or enthusiastic you are. They just want their money or they come and take everything away. And then you never get to Burbank, California. You just get hungry. And bitter. And then you drink yourself to death or you wind up in an insane asylum or rotting under a bridge someplace and then God knows where else.

Ruby sat up straight again and wiped her eyes until the sleeves of her gown were cold and wet.

Announcer #2:
We are ready now to take you to the Princeton Observatory at Princeton where Carl Phillips, our commentator, will interview Professor Richard Pierson, famous astronomer. We take you now to Princeton, New Jersey.

Tom was almost to town now. He slowed the car and turned the volume back up. Princeton men were on the case—and he wanted to hear what they thought about "regular explosions of incandescent gas on the planet Mars."

Phillips:
Good evening, ladies and gentlemen. This is Carl Phillips, speaking to you from the observatory at Princeton. I am standing in a large semi-circular room, pitch black except for an oblong split in the ceiling. Through this opening I can see a sprinkling of stars that cast a kind of frosty glow over the intricate mechanism of the huge telescope. The ticking sound you hear is the vibration of the clockwork. Professor Pierson stands directly above me on a small platform, peering through the giant lens. I ask you to be patient, ladies and gentlemen, during any delay that may arise during our interview. Beside his ceaseless watch of the heavens, Professor Pierson may be interrupted by telephone or other communications. During this period he is in constant touch with the astronomical centers of the world...Professor, may I begin our questions?

Pierson:
At any time, Mr. Phillips.

Phillips:
Professor, would you please tell our radio audience exactly what you see as you observe the planet Mars through your telescope?

Pierson:
Nothing unusual at the moment, Mr. Phillips. A red disk swimming in a blue sea. Transverse stripes across the disk. Quite distinct now because Mars happens to be at the point nearest the earth...in opposition, as we call it.

Phillips:
In your opinion, what do these transverse stripes signify, Professor Pierson?

Pierson:
Not canals, I can assure you, Mr. Phillips, although that's the popular conjecture of those who imagine Mars to be inhabited. From a scientific viewpoint the stripes are merely the result of atmospheric conditions peculiar to the planet.

Phillips:
Then you're quite convinced as a scientist that living intelligence as we know it does not exist on Mars?

Pierson:
I should say the chances against it are a thousand to one.

Phillips:
And yet how do you account for these gas eruptions occurring on the surface of the planet at regular intervals?

Pierson:
Mr. Phillips, I cannot account for it.

Phillips:
By the way, Professor, for the benefit of our listeners, how far is Mars from the earth?

Pierson:
Approximately forty million miles.

Phillips:
Well, that seems a safe enough distance.

Phillips:
Just a moment, ladies & gentlemen, someone has just handed Professor Pierson a message. While he reads it, let me remind you that we are speaking to you from the observatory in Princeton, New Jersey, where the world-famous astronomer, Professor Pierson...One moment, please. Professor Pierson has passed me a message which he has just received...Professor, may I read the message to the listening audience?

Pierson:
Certainly, Mr. Phillips.

Phillips:
Ladies & Gentlemen, I shall read you a wire addressed to Professor Pierson from Dr. Gray of the Natural History Museum, New York. "9:15 PM, eastern standard time. Seismograph registered shock of almost earthquake intensity occurring within a radius of twenty miles of Princeton. Please investigate. Signed, Lloyd Gray, Chief of Astronomical Division."... Professor Pierson, could this occurrence possibly have something to do with the disturbances observed on the planet Mars?

Pierson:
Hardly, Mr. Phillips. This is probably a meteorite of unusual size and its arrival at this

particular time is merely a coincidence. However, we shall conduct a search, as soon as daylight permits.

Phillips:
Thank you, Professor. Ladies & Gentlemen, for the past ten minutes we've been speaking to you from the observatory at Princeton, bringing you a special interview with Professor Pierson, noted astronomer. This is Carl Phillips speaking. We now return you to our New York studio.
(Fade in piano playing)

At that moment a horn startled Tom from behind. A truck was on his tailgate; he realized that he'd been listening so intently that he'd unconsciously slowed the A-Model to a crawl. Noticing that he had reached the city limits of Hackettstown, he sped up quickly and pulled out of the way.

A meteorite near Princeton. That's less than 60 miles from here! And explosions like gunfire on Mars. By God, this is strange! Tom had been keeping up with things like this since he was a kid, but he had never...Well, surely when they get somebody down there they'll see...what would they see?

Announcer #2:
Ladies & Gentlemen, here is the latest bulletin from the Intercontinental Radio News. Montreal, Canada: Professor Morse of McGill University reports observing a total of three explosions on the planet Mars, between the hours of 7:45 PM and 9:20 PM, eastern standard time. This confirms earlier reports received from American observatories. Now, nearer home, comes a special announcement from Trenton, New Jersey. It is reported that at 8:50 PM, a huge flaming object, believed to be a meteorite, fell on a farm in the neighborhood of Grovers Mill, New Jersey, twenty-two miles from Trenton.

Twenty-two miles from Trenton? Hell, that's right in our neighborhood!

...the flash in the sky was visible within a radius of several hundred miles and the noise of the impact was heard as far north as Elizabeth.

Tom hadn't noticed a flash, but...

...We have dispatched a special mobile unit to the scene, and we will have our commentator, Mr. Phillips, give you a word description as soon as he can reach there from Princeton. In the meantime, we take you to the Hotel Martinet in Brooklyn, where Bobby Millette and his orchestra are offering a program of dance music.

(Swing band interlude)

Just what in blazes was this all about? Tom caught himself jumping to conclusions. He had an open mind when it came to the topic of life on the other planets. In fact, the kids in school had always laughed and called him "Buck Rogers" over it. But...doggone it, he wasn't *screwy*. There had to be a simpler explanation for all this...even if he couldn't happen to think of one right now.

He pulled up to another stop light, this one on Main Street just down from the movie house. It changed to green and he suddenly realized that he'd forgotten where he was going.

Announcer #2:
We now take you to Grovers Mill, New Jersey.
(Crowd noises...police sirens)

Tom got hooted again with another horn. A big Packard filled his rear-view mirror for a few seconds before surging ahead to pass with obvious irritation.

Phillips:
Ladies & Gentlemen, this is Carl Phillips again, at the Wilmuth farm, Grovers Mill, New Jersey. Professor Pierson and myself made the eleven miles from Princeton in ten minutes. Well, I...I hardly know where to begin, to paint for you a word picture of the strange scene before my eyes, like something out of a modern Arabian Nights. Well, I just got here. I haven't had a chance to look around yet. I guess that's it. Yes, I guess that's the...thing directly in front of me, half buried in a vast pit. Must have struck with terrific force. The ground is covered with splinters of a tree it must have struck on its way down. What I can see of the...object itself doesn't look very much like a meteor, at least not the meteors I've seen. It looks more like a huge cylinder...

A cylinder? *Judas Priest!* What...what *kind* of a cylinder?

...It has a diameter of...what would you say, Professor Pierson?

Pierson (Off):
About thirty yards.

Phillips:
About thirty yards...The metal on the sheath is...well, I've never seen anything like it. The color is sort of yellowish-white. Curious spectators now are pressing close to the object in spite of the efforts of the police to keep them back. They're getting in front of my line of

vision. Would you mind standing on one side, please?

Policeman:
One side, there, one side.

This...this is the most fantastic thing I've ever...Tom realized he was going to have to stop somewhere just to listen. He noticed he was passing Garfield High School—his old alma mater. He quickly turned into the drive and then rolled to a stop in the empty gravel parking lot. He shut off the engine but left the switch on. The radio sounded out loud and clear across the stillness of the moonlit schoolyard.

Phillips:
While the policemen are pushing the crowd back, here's Mr. Wilmuth, owner of the farm here. He may have some interesting facts to add...Mr. Wilmuth, would you please tell the radio audience as much as you remember of this rather unusual visitor that dropped in your back yard? Step closer please. Ladies and gentlemen, this is Mr. Wilmuth.

Wilmuth:
I was listenin' to the radio.

Phillips:
Closer and louder, please.

Wilmuth:
Pardon me!

Phillips:
Louder, please, and closer.

As the announcer tried to interview the farmer Tom's mind raced ahead. Can that...that cylinder, as they called it...could it really be some kind of airship...or space shell...or whatever...from Mars? That would be...*astounding.* Why, there might even be someone alive inside of it! My God, think of it! Tom caught himself up. Take it easy, friend. We've got to think this out calmly. If those explosions on Mars were cylinders like this one, being shot into interplanetary space, then...

Waitasecond. This cylinder report came just a few minutes after the first word of the sightings on Mars. Surely nothing could cross forty million miles of ether in fifteen minutes!

Unless...unless the explosions we saw tonight weren't the first ones. The radio said that a *series* of explosions was seen. We might easily have missed seeing the first ones! The only reason the astronomers are looking at

Mars at all right now is that it's so close...in *opposition*, as that Pearson fellow said. If that's so then...well, this Grover's Mill thing might have left Mars weeks—even months ago. Which would *mean*...which would mean that there might be dozens of these things on the way. Why? For what purpose? If there are people alive on Mars, what would they come to earth for? To explore? Then what? What have we Earthmen always done after exploring a new world?

Colonized it. Conquered and colonized it...

Hell's bells. What am I thinking of? Tom shook his head as if to clear his brain. What a bunch of nonsense. Invaders from Mars. That's just the sort of thing everyone expects me to come up with, I guess—monsters from Outer Space.Well, I'm damned if I'll give them the satisfaction. Like I said before, there's got to be a logical explanation. I'm sure these fellows from Princeton will figure it out.

Phillips:
...Ladies and gentlemen, you've just heard Mr. Wilmuth, owner of the farm where this thing has fallen. I wish I could convey the atmosphere...the background of this...fantastic scene. Hundreds of cars are parked in a field in back of us. Police are trying to rope off the roadway leading into the farm. But it's no use. They're breaking right through. Their headlights throw an enormous spot on the pit where the object's half buried. Some of the more daring souls are venturing near the edge. Their silhouettes stand out against the metal sheen.
(Faint humming sound)

Ruby certainly wasn't dozing anymore. A planet (or something) colliding with Trenton was serious business. Her sister lived in Trenton.

She turned a light on, then picked up the telephone and jiggled the hook impatiently.

"...Number please..."

"Trenton 4833."

There was a long pause. Across the room, she could still hear the radio.

Phillips:
...One man wants to touch the thing...he's having an argument with a policeman. The policeman wins...

"...Sorry, all Trenton lines are busy, ma'am."

"Busy?"

"Yes ma'am. Have been for the last 15 minutes or so. Please try your call again later."

"Is it because of the meteor?"

"Meteor?"

"You know, this comet thing in Granger's Mill, or wherever. Haven't you heard?"

"...I'm sure I don't know what you mean, ma'am. Please try again later."

Irritated, Ruby hung up. She supposed that everything was all right with her sister; after all, the radio hadn't yet said anything about anyone hurt or killed. Still...she didn't know much about meteors...if they might be dangerous or something. Tom would know.

From the bedroom she heard the baby begin to stir.

Phillips:
Now, ladies and gentlemen, there's something I haven't mentioned in all this excitement, but it's becoming more distinct. Perhaps you've caught it already on your radio. Listen: (long pause)...Do you hear it? It's a curious humming sound that seems to be coming from inside the object. I'll move the microphone nearer. Here. (Pause)

Tom, still sitting in his car in the parking lot, was unconsciously leaning forward toward the radio, hungrily straining to hear and evaluate every sound, literally on the edge of his seat and gripping the wheel tightly. He thought he could just hear the faint humming the man talked about—a low, electric moan. This Professor Pierson...what was it he'd said? "The chances of anything coming from Mars are a thousand to one?" Long odds to be sure. But once a thing has actually *happened*...then odds don't matter, do they?

Phillips:
Now we're not more than twenty-five feet away. Can you hear it? Oh, Professor Pierson!

Pierson:
Yes, Mr. Phillips?

Phillips:
Can you tell us the meaning of that scraping noise inside the thing?

Pierson:
Possibly the unequal cooling of its surface.

Phillips:
Do you still think it's a meteor, Professor?

Pierson:
I don't know what to think. The metal casing is definitely extraterrestrial...not found on

this earth. Friction with the earth's atmosphere usually tears holes in a meteorite. This thing is smooth and, as you can see, of cylindrical shape.

...Not found on this earth, he says. Dear God. I wonder if...

Phillips:
Just a minute! Something's happening! Ladies and gentlemen, this is terrific! This end of the thing is beginning to flake off! The top is beginning to rotate like a screw! The thing must be hollow!

Voices:
She's a movin'!

Look, the darn thing's unscrewing!

Keep back, there! Keep back, I tell you!

Maybe there's men in it trying to escape!

It's red hot, they'll burn to a cinder!

Keep back there. Keep those idiots back!

(Suddenly the clanking sound of a huge piece of falling metal)

Voices:
She's off! The top's loose!

Look out there! Stand back!

Phillips:
Ladies and gentlemen, this is the most terrifying thing I have ever witnessed...Wait a minute! Someone's crawling out of the hollow top. Someone or...something. I can see peering out of that black hole two luminous disks...are they eyes? It might be a face. It might be...
(Shout of awe from the crowd)

Phillips:
Good heavens, something's wriggling out of the shadow like a gray snake. Now it's another one, and another. They look like tentacles to me. There, I can see the thing's body. It's large as a bear and it glistens like wet leather. But that face. It...it's indescribable. I can hardly force myself to keep looking at it. The eyes are black and gleam like a serpent. The mouth is V-shaped with saliva dripping from its rimless lips

that seem to quiver and pulsate. The monster or whatever it is can hardly move. It seems weighed down by...possibly gravity or something. The thing's raising up. The crowd falls back. They've seen enough. This is the most extraordinary experience. I can't find words...I'm pulling this microphone with me as I talk. I'll have to stop the description until I've taken a new position. Hold on, will you please, I'll be back in a minute. (Fade into piano)

Announcer #2:
We are bringing you an eyewitness account of what's happening on the Wilmuth farm, Grovers Mill, New Jersey...

The old black Ford roared out of the school parking lot with a vigor that belied its age, sending showers of gravel scattering out into the street. Tom covered the two-and-a-half remaining blocks to the Silver Grill in mere seconds. There would be a crowd there. People. They'd have the radio on, surely. He had to find someone...talk to *someone.* He didn't want to listen to any more of this alone.

Back at Tom's house—the one that cost him $35 a month that he couldn't really afford—his wife Ruby rocked their whimpering child in her arms and wept. She didn't understand any of this. None of it made any sense. But *Tom*...he would understand. Tom would explain it to her. He'd know what to do. But Tom was gone. And she didn't know where he was or when he was coming back.

Announcer #2:
We now return you to Carl Phillips at Grovers Mill...

The glass door of the diner flew open; a bell rang and the cold October wind poured through for a moment. Tom Loudermilk rushed in, looking for other humans.

Just as he'd expected, the eatery was filled to capacity, and the radiowas on. But Sunday dinner--the baked chicken special with mashed potatoes—sat half eaten on a dozen different plates as most of the customers stood crowded up to the counter listening to the voice of Carl Phillips.

Phillips:
Ladies and gentlemen (Am I on?). Ladies and gentlemen, here I am, back of a stone wall that adjoins Mr. Wilmuth's garden. From here I get a sweep of the whole scene. I'll give you every detail as long as I can talk. As long as I can see...

"How long have you been listening?" Tom blurted, to no one in particular.

He was soundly shushed by the cook, who was standing beside the radio with one hand resting on the volume control. Looking around, Tom saw two or three local families, several fellows from the mill, and two truck drivers stopped for supper on the way to Scranton. Rita Daniels was there too, as expected. She stood near the cash register, ignoring her customers, looking only at the blank face of the radio set. She was exactly as Tom remembered her but wearing an indescribable expression; she looked like a disoriented bunny rabbit caught in a trap. She didn't notice Tom. He paused a moment and then took the nearest available seat.

Phillips:
...More state police have arrived. They're drawing up a cordon in front of the pit, about thirty of them. No need to push the crowd back now. They're willing to keep their distance. The captain is conferring with someone. We can't see who. Oh yes, I believe it's Professor Pierson. Yes, it is. Now they've parted. The professor moves around one side, studying the object, while the captain and two policemen advance with something in their hands. I can see it now. It's a white handkerchief tied to a pole...a flag of truce. If those creatures know what that means...what anything means! Wait! Something's happening! (Hissing sound followed by a humming that increases in intensity)

A humped shape is rising out of the pit. I can make out a small beam of light against a mirror. What's that? There's a jet of flame springing from that mirror, and it leaps right at the advancing men. It strikes them head on! Good lord, they're turning into flame! (Screams and unearthly shrieks)

Now the whole field's caught fire. (Explosion) The woods...the barns...the gas tanks of automobiles...it's spreading everywhere. It's coming this way. About twenty yards to my right...

(Crash of microphone...then a long, dead silence)

"Jesus and Mary..." whispered the Cook.

"I...I never...that's the worst thing I ever heard," said someone, from out of one of the booths.

"My God," said one of the family men, hoarsely. "Was that for real?"

Announcer #2:
Ladies and gentlemen, due to circumstances beyond our control, we are unable to continue the broadcast from Grovers Mill. Evidently there's some difficulty with our field transmission. However, we will return to that point at the earliest opportunity. In the meantime, we have a late bulletin from San Diego, California. Professor Indellkoffer, speaking at a dinner of the California Astronomical Society, expressed the opinion that

the explosions on Mars are undoubtedly nothing more that severe volcanic eruptions on the surface of the planet. We continue now with our piano interlude...

"Volcanic eruptions!" Tom stood and cried out. "Well, the damn fool hasn't been listening to the radio, that's for sure!"

Rita spotted Tom for the first time. She recognized him dully, and then tried to smile but failed. Their eyes met. Hers seemed to say "Do you understand any of this?" Tom was afraid that he did. Every horrific thing he'd ever read about in *Weird Tales* or *Startling Stories*, every whopper about a bug-eyed monstrosity or a bubbling brainiac from beyond, was now buzzing in his head like a hangover...and he'd read some *lulus*.

Announcer #2:
Ladies and gentlemen, I have just been handed a message that came in from Grovers Mill by telephone. Just a moment. At least forty people, including six state troopers lie dead in a field east of the village of Grovers Mill, their bodies burned and distorted beyond all possible recognition. The next voice you hear will be that of Brigadier General Montgomery Smith, commander of the state militia at Trenton, New Jersey.

Smith:
I have been requested by the governor of New Jersey to place the counties of Mercer and Middlesex as far west as Princeton, and east to Jamesburg, under martial law. No one will be permitted to enter this area except by special pass issued by state or military authorities. Four companies of state militia are proceeding from Trenton to Grovers Mill, and will aid in the evacuation of homes within the range of military operations. Thank you.

Announcer:
You have just been listening to General Montgomery Smith, commanding the state militia at Trenton. In the meantime, further details of the catastrophe at Grovers Mill are coming in. The strange creatures after unleashing their deadly assault, crawled back in their pit and made no attempt to prevent the efforts of the firemen to recover the bodies and extinguish the fire. Combined fire departments of Mercer County are fighting the flames which menace the entire countryside.

We have been unable to establish any contact with our mobile unit at Grovers Mill, but we hope to be able to return you there at the earliest possible moment. In the meantime we take you uh, just one moment please.
(Long pause)

(Whisper) Ladies and gentlemen, I have just been informed that we have finally established communication with an eyewitness of the tragedy. Professor Pierson has been located at a farmhouse near Grovers Mill where he has established an emergency

observation post. As a scientist, he will give you his explanation of the calamity. The next voice you hear will be that of Professor Pierson, brought to you by direct wire. Professor Pierson.

Pierson:
Of the creatures in the rocket cylinder at Grovers Mill, I can give you no authoritative information either as to their nature, their origin, or their purposes here on earth. Of their destructive instrument I might venture some conjectural explanation. For want of a better term, I shall refer to the mysterious weapon as a heat ray. It's all too evident that these creatures have scientific knowledge far in advance of our own. It is my guess that in some way they are able to generate an intense heat in a chamber of practically absolute nonconductivity. This intense heat they project in a parallel beam against any object they choose, by means of a polished parabolic mirror of unknown composition, much as the mirror of a lighthouse projects a beam of light. That is my conjecture of the origin of the heat ray.

Announcer #2:
Thank you, Professor Pierson. Ladies and gentlemen, here is a bulletin from Trenton. It is a brief statement informing us that the charred body of Carl Phillips has been identified in a Trenton hospital.

A low groan came up from several diner patrons. Then a voice called out.

"Charlie?"

"Yeah?" the Cook answered.

"Can I use your phone?" It was one of the truck drivers. "I got family in New Brunswick..."

"New Brunswick? Uh...right. Sure. Here ya go."

Family. He thinks...he *realizes* that his family is in danger. With the force of a hammer blow to the head, Tom thought of Ruby.

Announcer #2:
...Now here's another bulletin from Washington D.C.
Office of the director of the National Red Cross reports ten units of Red Cross emergency workers have been assigned to the headquarters of the state militia stationed outside of Grovers Mill, New Jersey. Here's a bulletin from state police, Princeton Junction: The fires at Grovers Mill and vicinity are now under control. Scouts report all quiet in the pit, and no sign of life appearing from the mouth of the cylinder...And now, ladies and gentlemen, we have a special statement from Mr. Harry McDonald, vice-president in charge of operations.

McDonald:
We have received a request from the militia at Trenton to place at their disposal our

entire broadcasting facilities. In view of the gravity of the situation, and believing that radio has a definite responsibility to serve in the public interest at all times, we are turning over our facilities to the state militia at Trenton.

One of the fathers turned to his wife.

"C'mon. Let's go home."

Ernie Fields, one of the mill workers Tom had recognized, likewise reached for his hat.

"I better get home too. My wife's all by herself."

Behind the counter, the truck driver could be overheard at the telephone.

"Whatta ya mean all the lines are jammed?—Are you sure they're not *down*?—Well, when can I get through?—Listen, this is my mother we're talkin' about!—Well, fine, dammit, I'll just get in the truck and come down there!"

He slammed the earpiece down angrily.

Rita Daniels stepped over to Tom's seat by the door.

"Tom...I haven't seen you in so long..."

Tom said nothing.

"God, Tom do you think all of this is for real?"

"Well, we...we heard it for ourselves, didn't we? I wouldn't have believed it either..."

"Well, listen, you don't think we're in any danger way out here do you?"

"I...don't know what to think anymore."

Announcer:
We now take you to the field headquarters of the state militia near Grovers Mill, New Jersey.

Captain:
This is Captain Lansing of the signal corps, attached to the state militia now engaged in military operations in the vicinity of Grovers Mill. Situation arising from the reported presence of certain individuals of unidentified nature is now under complete control.

The cylindrical object which lies in a pit directly below our position is surrounded on all sides by eight battalions of infantry, without heavy field-pieces, but adequately armed with rifles and machine guns...

Ruby was on the brink of complete panic. The baby was crying loudly now, making it difficult to hear what was being said on the other end of the telephone line.

"What? I can't hear you!"

"I said that there's nothing we can do for you but to tell you to stay inside and keep your doors locked! We don't know any more about this than you."

"Well, you're the police aren't you?"

"Listen lady. I've had fifty calls in the last ten minutes just like this one. We're trying to get in touch with State Police headquarters but every long-distance line is jammed with callers like you!"

"Okay, look," she begged, her voice breaking into a plaintive childlike plea as she struggled to keep some little self-control. "We're all alone here. My husband's...away. And..I just don't want anything to happen to *my baby...*"

"I'm sorry, I didn't... Look, don't cry sweetheart. I'll call you back as soon as we know something and...until then I'll send an officer by as soon as one gets free."

"Thank you."

Out in the parking lot of the Silver Grill, Rita followed Tom to his car. The wind seemed colder now, the air bitter rather than bracing.

"Tom, I'm afraid."

"...Me, too."

"Where are you going?"

"I...need to get back home. You know...Ruby and the baby."

Across the way, the truck driver's rig roared to life. Tom heard the radio inside come on as the big machine rumbled out of the lot and disappeared onto the southbound road out of town. Now, somewhere in the distance, he and Rita noticed that they could hear the eerie wail of a police siren.

"Tom."

"Yeah?"

"Why did you come here tonight?"

"I...uh..."

At that moment a black Chevrolet came screaming past the diner—also on the road out of town. Tom guessed it must have been doing at least 80. It, too, disappeared into the night and then the siren could be heard again. Or maybe it was two sirens now, one on either end of town.

"Tom?"

Rita was close now. She'd left her sweater inside and was holding her arms crossed in front of her chest against the chill. Tom thought that perhaps she was even prettier than he had remembered.

"You were about to say..." she continued.

"...I came in for the special."

"The what...?"

"The baked chicken—with mashed potatoes."

"Oh."

They both jumped at what sounded like a woman's scream, coming from an apartment house down the avenue. Everywhere in town it seemed, lights were going on and people were coming out into the street.

"Listen, Rita, do you have any boyfriends?"

"Yeah. One or two. You know."

"Well, pick out a nice one, okay? One that will be good to you?"

"All right, Tom."

The door of the diner flew open. The other truck driver rushed out. As he passed Tom and Rita he spoke.

"The Army's goin' in. I'm going back to New York... They might call up my Guard Unit."

Tom opened the door of his car and dropped behind the wheel. He cranked the engine and then switched the radio back on.

Captain:
... One of the companies is deploying to the left flank. A quick thrust and it will all be over. Now wait a minute! I see something on top of the cylinder. No, it's nothing but a shadow. Now the troops are on the edge of the Wilmuth farm. Seven thousand armed men closing in on an old metal tube. Wait, that wasn't a shadow! It's something moving...solid metal...kind of a shieldlike affair rising up out of the cylinder...It's going higher and higher. Why, it's standing on legs... actually rearing up on a sort of metal framework. Now it's reaching above the trees and the searchlights are on it! Hold on!...

The captain's voice broke off. The broadcast seemed to collapse into confusion. Dead air. The silence was deafening.

"Goodbye Rita. Take care of yourself tonight."

"G'bye Tom."

Announcer #2:
Ladies and gentlemen, I have a grave announcement to make. Incredible as it may seem, both the observations of science and the evidence of our eyes lead to the inescapable assumption that those strange beings who landed in the Jersey farmlands tonight are the vanguard of an invading army from the planet Mars. The battle which took place tonight at Grovers Mill has ended in one of the most startling defeats ever suffered by an army in modern times; seven thousand men armed with rifles and machine guns pitted against a single fighting machine of the invaders from Mars. One hundred and twenty known survivors. The rest strewn over the battle area from Grovers Mill to Plainsboro crushed and trampled to death under the metal feet of the monster, or burned to cinders by its heat ray. The monster is now in control of the middle section of New Jersey and has effectively cut the state through its center. Communication lines are down from Pennsylvania to the Atlantic Ocean. Railroad tracks are torn and service from New York to Philadelphia discontinued except routing some of the trains through Allentown and Phoenixville.

Highways to the north, south, and west are clogged with frantic human traffic. Police and army reserves are unable to control the mad flight. By morning the fugitives will have swelled Philadelphia, Camden and Trenton, it is estimated, to twice their normal population...

Tom's drive out of Hackettstown was nothing short of harrowing. The roads were filling rapidly and nobody paid the slightest attention to speed limits, road signs, stop lights, or any other form of traffic regulation. Everywhere he saw visible proof that a war of some kind had indeed begun. Every light within the city limits was blazing. The sidewalks were crowded with people; some of them running, some of them yelling at each other in excited clumps, some of them milling about aimlessly, many of them armed with shotguns and hunting rifles. At the schoolyard where he'd stopped on the way in, a group of youths had started a bonfire. Somewhere nearby, a churchbell was ringing.

When he reached the Hwy. 73 intersection—where he'd calmly watched the autumn leaves drifting down the road not long ago—a policeman stood in the middle of the road, caught between Tom's headlights and a huge orange pillar of fire that silhouetted him from behind. He authoritatively waved Tom's car to a stop. Closer now, Tom could see that the flames were roaring up out of an overturned farm truck which seemed to have buried its nose in the low shoulder of Route 9 just past the filling station. Its load of about 200 large pumpkins lay scattered for 50 yards in a broken, shattered trail of pulp and seeds. Red lights played over the scene hypnotically; in addition to the policeman's squad car, a fire truck had arrived and a team of men were unrolling hoses. Nearby, a power pole, sheared off at the base, lay tangled in web of sparking, overextended electric lines.

"What happened?"

The cop stepped alongside, raising his voice to be heard..

"Some fool ran him off the road. Driver's okay. Says the guy must have been a maniac...headed east in an Oldsmobile like a bat outta hell."

"Have you any news from downstate... about the Martians?"

"Martians?...Son, have you actually *seen* any Martians?"

"No, I haven't."

"Nobody has. Nobody that I can find anyway. All I know is that everybody's suddenly gone nuts and they all blame it on Martians."

"The radio says..."

"I know what the radio says. A planetoid or something's down in Mercer county. All I know is that nothing's happening up here that couldn't be explained with a few empty whiskey bottles, if we could find any. Anyhow, I'd get off the roads if I were you...Where you headed?"

"...uh, just a few more miles. Lumberton Road."

"Well, watch it. This down pole's got the lights off from here to Vienna."

"To *Vienna?*"

Tom thought of Ruby and the baby. They'd be sitting alone in the dark. God, what the hell had he been thinking of, leaving them there like that?

Announcer #2:
...At this time martial law prevails throughout New Jersey and eastern Pennsylvania. We take you now to Washington for a special broadcast on the National Emergency...the Secretary of the Interior...

Secretary:
Citizens of the nation: I shall not try to conceal the gravity of the situation that confronts the country, nor the concern of your government in protecting the lives and property of its people. However, I wish to impress upon you private citizens and public officials, all of you the urgent need of calm and resourceful action. Fortunately, this formidable enemy is still confined to a relatively small area, and we may place our faith in the military forces to keep them there. In the meantime placing our faith in God we must continue the performance of our duties each and every one of us, so that we may confront this destructive adversary with a nation united, courageous, and consecrated to the preservation of human supremacy on this earth. I thank you.

Announcer:
You have just heard the Secretary of the Interior speaking from Washington...

"Our Father, which art in heaven. Hallowed be thy name..."

Ruby had bitten her hand when the lights went out to keep from screaming. She knew she had to keep herself together for the baby's sake. Then she had frantically scrambled through an old chest of drawers to find the cheap little rosary she'd been given at her confirmation. She knelt against Tom's old armchair, not far from the now silent radio, clutching their little girl to her breast. The house was very dark but any minute she expected to see--out the back window--the glow of red flames on the southern horizon.

"Hail Mary, full of grace. The Lord is with thee..."

Ruby and Tom rarely went to church. There seemed so little need back when everything was normal, back when they had life all figured out...back when Mars was only an orange dot in Tom's old telescope. But now...well, perhaps if there really *are* Martians and spaceships and death-rays after all...then perhaps God and Jesus and Heaven are really there too…

"Glory be to the Father, and to the Son, and to the Holy Ghost; as it was in the beginning, is now, and ever shall be, world without end."

Ruby was surprised that she still remembered the prayers.

Announcer:
...Bulletins too numerous to read are piling up in the studio here. We are informed that the central portion of New Jersey is blacked out from radio communications due to the effect of the heat ray upon power lines and electrical equipment. Here is a special bulletin from New York. Cables received from English, French, German scientific bodies offering assistance. Astronomers report continued gas outbursts on planet Mars. Majority voice opinion that enemy will be reinforced by additional rocket machines. Attempts made to locate Professor Pierson of Princeton, who has observed Martians at close range.
Langham Field, Virginia: scouting planes report three Martian machines visible above treetops, moving north toward Somerville with population fleeing ahead of them. Heat ray not in use; although advancing at express train speed the invaders pick their way carefully. They seem to be making conscious effort to avoid destruction of cities and countryside. However, they stop to uproot power lines, bridges, and railroad tracks. Their apparent objective is to crush resistance, paralyze communication, and disorganize human society.
Here is a bulletin from Basking Ridge, New Jersey: Coon hunters have stumbled on a second cylinder similar to the first embedded in the great swamp twenty miles south of Morristown. U.S. Army fieldpieces are proceeding from Newark to blow up second invading unit before cylinder can be opened and the fighting machine rigged. They are taking up position in the foothills of Watchung Mountains. Another bulletin from Langham Field, Virginia: Scouting planes report enemy machines, now three in number, increasing speed northward kicking over houses and trees in their evident haste to form a conjunction with their allies south of Morristown. Machines also sighted by telephone operator east of Middlesex within ten miles of Plainfield...

Ten miles from Plainfield. And Tom was still two miles from home. For the first time, it occurred to him that he might never see Ruby again.

Instantly, he was overwhelmed with the most intense feelings of love for her that he had ever had. The memory of her smile, of the pitiful little way her face would screw up just before she cried over some little something, of the way her voice went off key when she sang to the baby. All these things seemed, now that they were perhaps lost forever, like half-remembered images from some previous existence in paradise. Tom found his eyes welling up with hot, salty tears. That he could ever have been unhappy with her made him feel...ashamed.

Only another mile or two. Surely God would allow him another mile or two. Then, at least, he could be with Ruby just one more time—take her into his arms and swear to her that whatever happened after that he was content to face.

And then the right front tire blew.

The car was yanked violently off the edge of the pavement. Tom wrestled with the wheel as the whole vehicle shuddered as if it were being driven over railroad ties. He had enough presence of mind left not to stomp the brakes, but manhandled the wheel gradually to the left and back up onto the road where it finally coasted sloppily to a halt. He shut the engine off and sat completely still behind the wheel for a full minute.

He'd known that the tire was about ready to go. Any day, in fact. Tires are one of the things that have to wait when you can't pay the bills as it is. But now...now he cursed himself for it. He flung the door open and stepped out into the night.

The wind had died down again; the roadside was completely still. There was nothing along this stretch but woods on either side of the highway. The moon was beginning to rise over the trees in the southeast. Tom knew this road pretty well—he'd been going up and down it most of his life—and he knew he was still a good mile-and-a-half from home.

"Dammit!"

He kicked the side of the flat tire and set the whole car rocking. There was a suppressed sob in his voice.

"Damn! God-da..."

He'd started to curse—and then caught himself. It now seemed quite possible that he would not live through the night. Perhaps if he was going to call on God he'd better do it in a different tone of voice.

He opened the trunk and pulled out a rusty jack, a lug wrench, and a pathetic old spare not a bit better than the tire that just blew. He hastily propped the jack under the front bumper and then stopped to turn the radio back on before dropping to his knees in the dust next to the affected wheel.

(Fading in...sound of airplane motor)
Commander:
Army bombing plane, V-8 43, off Bayonne, New Jersey, Lt. Voght, commanding eight bombers. Reporting to Commander Fairfax, Langham Field...This is Voght, reporting to Commander Fairfax, Langham Field...Enemy tripod machines now in sight. Reinforced by three machines from the Morristown cylinder...Six altogether. One machine partially crippled. Believed hit by shell from army gun in Watchung Mountains. Guns now appear silent. A heavy black fog hanging close to the earth...of extreme density, nature unknown. No sign of heat ray. Enemy now turns east, crossing Passaic River into the Jersey marshes. Another straddles the Pulaski Skyway. Evident objective is New York City. They're pushing down a high-tension power station. The machines are close together now, and we're ready to attack. Planes circling, ready to strike. A thousand yards and we'll be over the first - eight hundred yards...six hundred...four hundred...two hundred...There they go! The giant arm raised...Green flash! They're spraying us with flame! Two thousand feet. Engines are giving out. No chance to release bombs. Only one thing left...drop on them, plane and all. We're diving on the first one. Now the engines

gone! Eight...

Operator One:
This is Bayonne, New Jersey, calling Langham Field...
This is Bayonne, New Jersey, calling Langham Field...
Come in, please...come in, please...

They're on the ropes. The army's on the ropes.
It's the end of the world, isn't it?

Operator Two:
This is Langham Field...go ahead...

Operator One:
Eight army bombers in engagement with enemy tripod machines over Jersey flats. Engines incapacitated by heat ray. All crashed. One enemy machine destroyed. Enemy now discharging heavy black smoke in direction of…

Tom put all his weight behind the lug wrench, trying to start one of the rusty nuts unscrewing. Grunting, he thought he felt it begin to give...before a sharp snap rang out and both nut and bolt came off inside the wrench and sent him sprawling onto his hands.

Operator Three:
This is Newark, New Jersey...
This is Newark, New Jersey...
Warning! Poisonous black smoke pouring in from New Jersey marshes. Reaches South Street. Gas masks useless. Urge population to move into open spaces...automobiles use Routes 7, 23, 24...Avoid congested areas. Smoke now spreading over Raymond Boulevard...

Tom tried to dig the broken-off bolt out of the end of the wrench. He'd put so much force against it that the piece seemed welded in place. He noticed blood all over the back of his hand. Must have busted his knuckles against the wheel when the metal snapped...

Operator #4:
2X2L...calling CQ...
2X2L...calling CQ...
2X2L...calling 8X3R...
Come in, please...

Operator #5:
This is 8X3R...coming back at 2X2L.

Operator #4:
How's reception? How's reception? K, please. Where are you, 8X3R? What's the matter? Where are you?

"Jesus Christ!"

Tom pulled back and then sent the lug wrench whistling into the woods just as hard as he could throw. It rustled through the branches for a moment and then landed with a soft thud somewhere in complete darkness.

"Jesus Christ...Jesus..."

Tom fell against the hood of the car. The tears were flowing freely now.

"Jesus, if you're for real...if you're really out there...Help me. Help me to get home to Ruby. I...I know I don't deserve it. I was leaving her. I was leaving her of my own free will. Have mercy on me. Have mercy on us all..."

Announcer:
I'm speaking from the roof of Broadcasting Building, New York City. The bells you hear are ringing to warn the people to evacuate the city as the Martians approach. Estimated in last two hours three million people have moved out along the roads to the north, Hutchison River Parkway still kept open for motor traffic. Avoid bridges to Long Island...hopelessly jammed. All communication with Jersey shore closed ten minutes ago. No more defenses. Our army wiped out...artillery, air force, everything wiped out. This may be the last broadcast. We'll stay here to the end...People are holding service below us...in the cathedral.
(Voices singing hymns)
Now I look down the harbor. All manner of boats, overloaded with fleeing population, pulling out from docks.
(Sound of boat whistles)
Streets are all jammed. Noise in crowds like New Year's Eve in city. Wait a minute...Enemy now in sight above the Palisades. Five great machines. First one is crossing river. I can see it from here, wading the Hudson like a man wading through a brook...A bulletin's handed me...Martian cylinders are falling all over the country. One outside Buffalo, one in Chicago, St. Louis...seem to be timed and spaced...now the first machine reaches the shore. He stands watching, looking over the city. His steel, cowlish head is even with the skyscrapers. He waits for the others. They rise like a line of new towers on the city's west side...Now they're lifting there metal hands. This is the end now. Smoke comes out...black smoke drifting over the city. People in the streets see it now. They're running towards the East River...thousands of them, dropping in like rats. Now

the smoke's spreading faster. It's reached Times Square. People trying to run away from it, but it's no use. They're falling like flies. Now the smoke's crossing Sixth Avenue...Fifth Avenue...one hundred yards away...it's fifty feet...
(Silence)

Operator #4:
2X2L calling CQ...
2X2L calling CQ...
2X2L calling CQ...New York.
(Silence)
Isn't there anyone on the air?
Isn't there anyone...
(Silence)

Tom ran the rest of the way home. He was out of shape. His heart felt like it would crack and his side ached like a gunshot wound. But he ran the whole way. He didn't care. All he cared about was getting back to Ruby.

As he labored, he looked up occasionally at the frosty sky overhead. It gleamed with a million silvery lights. The fine black silhouettes made by the pines sketched sharp lines against the horizon—the horizon to which he continually for signs of the Martian advance. Twice he was passed by speeding autos headed in the other direction; they paid him no attention at all. The night was cold enough that he could see his own breath. His nose began to drip and his eyes stayed so wet that he could barely see at times. But in his mind's eye he could see everything—the ruined cities, the empty towns, the heaps of human carrion lying out in the sun. Here at last was Man's long overdue comeuppance. He had been, after all, only a big fish in a small pond. If indeed this is how the world ends...well, then Tom suddenly saw everything in a new light. He saw that he had spent his whole life looking to the future—always ransoming today to some glorious imaginary tomorrow. But now he knew the truth—that tomorrow doesn't matter. It never had. What had mattered were only those things which matter whether they continue or not.

Tom stopped only once. Coming around the last big bend before Lumberton Road he froze dead in his tracks. A patch of sky opened between the trees on his right and there, standing against the stars taller than the trees, stood a black, mechanical apparatus raised on three skeletal legs.

It was silent, completely still, and rigid. It looked as if it were poised to pounce—like a cat about to leap on a bird. Here it was. The black angel, the destroyer, in his own backyard. Tom's thoughts seemed to slow, to take on a dream-like clarity. This was it apparently. He would die now. No more wriggling on the hook. The moment of truth.

And then he squinted again...and recognized the old water tower...the one put up by the County Extension office...standing just where it had for ten years now.

Finally, he saw his own cheap little house up ahead.

It was entirely dark. A few steps closer and he saw that the front door stood wide open. The gaping hole it left looked like a bottomless pit.

Stumbling up the front steps he called out her name.

"Ruby?"

There was nothing.

"Ruby, where are you?"

He staggered into the inky interior, barking his shins on everything, crashing into the furniture.

"Ruby!"

He fumbled his way into the kitchen; a box of matches sat next to the stove. He struck one. The flickering yellow light fell dimly out into the house. He carried it slowly from room to room, from one end of the little crackerbox to the other. Nothing was out of place. Everything sat patiently for the wife and little girl who were not there. It made Tom think of those ghost ships you read about—when the sails hang limp and breakfast sits half-eaten in the mess but the crew is gone. And then the match burned his fingers.

The nearly absolute darkness collapsed back in on him. He stood for a moment in the very center of the living room. Then he fell heavily to the floor; first onto his knees, then onto his hands and knees.

He couldn't...wouldn't...imagine what had happened to them...to his child and his Ruby. He had imagined too much. He couldn't imagine at all anymore. It hurt to try. And so he simply knelt there...waiting for whatever was to come next...not particularly caring what it might be.

"Hello up there!"

The voice had an electric sound to it. Coming over a bullhorn, he thought.

"This is the police. Come on out, whoever you are."

Tom looked up from the floor. A bright light could be seen through the living room windows, playing across the front of the house.

"Look, someone reported you so you might as well come down."

Reported me? Tom rose unsteadily to his feet.

"We're not going to have any more of this looting, alright? So come on out before I come up there and get you..."

Moving to the front door, he was blinded by a cold, white searchlight springing up from the road. Putting one hand up against the glare, he stepped through the door out onto the porch. When he did, a voice cried out sharply.

"Tom!"

It was a woman's voice this time. In another second, Tom knew that it was Ruby.

"It's my husband!"

The searchlight dropped. Tom rushed forward, still blinded a little, nearly tumbling down the steps. Ruby rushed up with the baby, sobbing with relief.

"*Tom.*"

They fell into each other's embrace, a family again.

"Tom...oh, Tom...I thought...I don't know what I thought..."

Tom kissed her face repeatedly, then kissed the baby's face. He didn't speak. He didn't know what to say. Ruby looked up into his eyes.

"Sorry Mr. Loudermilk," came a voice from nearby. "Not long after the power went off—a few minutes after I picked your wife up—we got a report of a looter in your house."

"...Were you listening to the radio tonight, Tom?"

"I know...the Martians."

"It's all a hoax, darling."

"It's what...?"

"It's some kind of practical joke. Some kind of a play or something."

Tom pulled back to see her face clearly.

"What did you say?"

"There aren't any Martians. I said the whole thing's a mistake."

Looking around, Tom noticed a big squad car idling close at hand. The policeman snapped off the searchlight and stepped forward.

"That's right. The whole thing's a gag. And a pretty sick one, if you ask me."

"I...I can't believe it."

"I don't blame you. But listen..."

The officer turned back to his car and opened the door. In a few seconds, he had the radio inside playing Beethoven's Sixth.

"That's what's on 650. Now listen to this..."

He turned the dial. Static buzzed for a second before he landed on another station.

"And we hope you'll be sure to tune in again next week, when Edgar & Charlie's guests will be Dorothy Lamour, Benny Goodman..."

"Okay, that's Charlie McCarthy on NBC. Now back to CBS..."

Pierson:

...Suddenly, my eyes were attracted to the immense flock of black birds that hovered directly below me. They circled to the ground and there before my eyes, stark and silent, lay the Martians, with hungry birds pecking and tearing brown shreds of flesh from their dead bodies. Later when their bodies were examined in laboratories, it was found that

they were killed by the putrefactive and disease bacteria against which their systems were unprepared...slain, after all man's defenses had failed, by the humblest thing that God in His wisdom put upon this earth...

"They say the fellow behind it is named Welles..." the cop continued. "Orson Welles. Some kind of pointy-headed New York playwright. I guess he's having a good laugh on us rubes. They oughta string the bastard up if you ask me."

"...How's that?" Tom asked distractedly.

"I say, they ought to lynch the fool for doing a thing like that. You can't believe the trouble it's caused. We've got a full scale panic on our hands in this state. Never seen anything like it. I'll be up the rest of the night calming people down from here to the Pennsylvania border."

Tom turned his head. Ruby let him move away for a moment. He put his hands into his pockets and, turning his back, took a few steps away into the night.

After a minute or two, Ruby went to his side and spoke again,

"Tom?"

"Yes, sweetheart?"

"You're not angry?"

"...with Mr. Orson Welles?"

Tom reflected for a moment. The moon was up full now; he noticed that it cast a beautiful silvery glow across the front lawn of his fine $35-a-month house.

"No, honey, I don't guess I am."

"Panic's an ugly thing sometimes..." the officer interjected. "Brings out the truth, y'know. You find out what people are really like...deep down inside."

Ruby thought she could see a smile on Tom's lips.

"I hope you're right, officer."

Director:
This is Orson Welles, ladies and gentlemen, out of character to assure you that 'The War of the Worlds' has no further significance than as the holiday offering it was intended to be. The Mercury Theatre's own radio version of dressing up in a sheet and jumping out of a bush and saying Boo! Starting now, we couldn't soap all your windows and steal all your garden gates by tomorrow night...so we did the next best thing. We annihilated the world before your very ears, and utterly destroyed the Columbia Broadcasting System. You will be relieved, I hope, to learn that we didn't mean it, and that both institutions are still open for business. So good-bye everybody, and remember, please, for the next day or so, the terrible lesson you learned tonight. That grinning, glowing, globular invader of your living room is an inhabitant of the pumpkin patch, and if your doorbell rings and nobody's there, that was no Martian...it's Hallowe'en."

A Princeton University study commissioned in the aftermath of the *War of the Worlds* panic estimated that of the approximately 6 million people who listened to the program, at least 1,200,000 took the broadcast literally.

Originally published in Wonder #9, Winter 1994

ALSO BY ROD BENNETT

Four Witnesses: The Early Church in Her Owns Words

The Christus Experiment

Chesterton's America: A Distributist History of the United States

The Apostasy That Wasn't: The Extraordinary Story of the Unbreakable Early Church

For more information, visit Rod' author page at:
http://wonderboss.wix.com/christus

Made in the USA
Lexington, KY
20 September 2019